take this waltz

take this waltz

A Celebration
of Leonard Cohen

Edited by
Michael Fournier and Ken Norris

The Muses' Company/La Compagnie des Muses
Ste. Anne de Bellevue, Quebec
1994

Dépôt légal, Bibliothèque nationale du Québec
and The National Library of Canada, 4th Quarter 1994

Published by The Muses' Company/La Compagnie des Muses
P.O. Box 214
Ste. Anne de Bellevue, Quebec
H9X 3R9

Cover Photo by Christof Graf
Cover and interior design by Michael Fournier
Typeset in New Baskerville
Printed by Imprimerie d'Edition Marquis Ltée

The publisher gratefully acknowledges the financial assistance of the
Canada Council.

ISBN 0-919754-56-2

Canadian Cataloguing in Publication Data

Main entry under title:

Take this waltz: a celebration of Leonard Cohen

Includes index
ISBN 0-919754-56-2

1. Cohen, Leonard, 1934- –Criticism and
Interpretation. I. Norris, Ken, 1951-
II. Fournier, Michael, 1964-

PS8505.O22Z88 1994   C811´.54   C94-900517-7
PR9199.3.C57Z89 1994

Contents

Introduction

So far, the '90s have been a remarkable decade for Leonard Cohen. In 1991, *I'm Your Fan* was released—an album of Cohen covers performed by younger "alternative" artists such as R.E.M. and The Pixies, as well as some not so young, like Nick Cave and John Cale. In 1992, Cohen released *The Future*, arguably one of the strongest albums of his career. In the summer of 1993, he toured the world in support of that album, playing before audiences of screaming teens and smiling octogenarians. Late fall saw the publication of *Stranger Music: Selected Poems and Songs*. And as this book goes to press, he's just released his first live album in twenty years, a record of his '88 and '93 tours, and we can look forward to a second tribute album by various artists to be released later in the year. On the cusp of his seventh decade, Leonard Cohen's career is in as fine shape as it's ever been.

This book applauds the man's durability, his wit, his music and his words, celebrating his sixtieth birthday by offering some odd index of what people think of him, remember of him, want of him, and know of him. By no means is this book intended to mark closure of any kind—it's just that sixty is such a nice round number.

It's hard to refrain from quoting one of his discarded verses from "Jazz Police":

> I am coming back when I am sixty.
> I am coming back to take it all.
> Everybody hopes that I'll be filthy,
> But I will be like marble in the hall.

Prophetic words, but you were expecting maybe "Louie, Louie?" Of course, Leonard Cohen would be the first one to tell you that "Louie, Louie" is a really great song.

M.F. & K.N.
July 16, 1994

9

JOAN BAEZ

To Leonard Cohen on his 60th

Leonard,

I remember
1960 something
that ropey hotel restaurant
in the village
some man throwing up
in the phone booth
off the lobby
and you Leonard
king of
black predictions
harbinger of
a scorched earth
my dinner host
bemused
speaking in dark riddles
I didn't understand

Yet from your moonless dreams
did the Sisters of Mercy drift up
lovely and irreverent
perfumed and full of folly
and Suzanne
a careless ghost
pure as a young belief
beautiful as the new age
daughter of the dawn of Aquarius
the absent-minded seductress
hurling tote bags of goodness
to the dreamers on line
at Woodstock

and Joan of Arc
and Bernadette
and birds on wires and midnight choirs
so much beauty
from so much darkness
a gift
like wild grasses in the Hebrides
or the scent of the earth

1993
a song called Tacoma Trailer
played innocently
on my walkman
in Wurzburg Germany
while I watched
a snowstorm
tear past my window
in horizontal white splendor
predictably wondrous
when in disbelief I spotted
plain as life itself
a tattered little boy
struggling into the storm
and I brought him up
with my eyes
into the warmth
of my room
and into my arms

in 1993 Leonard
from your canopied dreams
came Yasha
who wrote these
unlikely lines
to your song of Tacoma Trailer

"Take these silver lakes from my eyes

I am ever so young
my knees are blue from the cold
and my hands are frozen

My name is Yasha
I come to you dying and offer these silver lakes
which for you will be dressed in summer
dreamlike under linden trees
blue and clear
and full of shining fish

. . . And I
I will lie down in the snow
and hear music of violins
and rich cellos
and I will die
this is the simplest
and what I expect . . . "

There is more
much more
to these writings of Yasha
and to all the other things
you have given to me
and to this century.

Happy 60th!

DOUGLAS BARBOUR

History: Manhattan—Montreal—Berlin

They had sentenced him. Me also, to over twenty long years. But of what. Boredom is for others, trying not to notice change. In the broken system, shift from without within. But I'm not coming not now no I'm changing 'coming' around to a reward for them. The first cocktail we could take: a Manhattan. Drunk then and we could take anything. Berlin perhaps.

I'm through being guided. Poems are by the way. A song is a signal enough, and in those days the stairway to heavens. You say I'm not only guided but it's by the text. This heretofore unacknowledged birthmark is language on parole. Remember: my razor cut skin. But now I'm a sucker guided through labyrinths by monks offering the revelation of beauty in and of itself. Let our politicians sell weapons. Let the first be last. We know that. Take off for Manhattan; sing loud then sing soft. We hear you take chances in Berlin.

I'd reread the novel. Really. Often, because I like it, a desire to learn how to live I guess. Something beside that? Well, there's you, that mystique, and baby, all the time I wondered. Talk about love; we talk about your version, how the body is part of and yet not it, your insistence on the spirit all dressed up and in there wearing your old and new clothes worn inside out. But someone might ask you if you can see something out beyond that horizon or coast line beyond its being there. You just keep moving across streets and through corridors down into the bowels of the station of the cross. I lost you but told them I saw you. Then much later I changed my story told someone else but you had disappeared so I went underground. Who told them that. Or you. But the photograph I took: oh that you was perfect and changed. One or more of the records. Yeah, those.

You sang from the tower, loved all audiences equally, even me it seemed. It was as good a time as a song written for a loser could provide. That's true but not in fact and even now it matters more that you're putting body in music, worried about the changing voice that charted how you and I and everyone were aging just as predicted. It wasn't might alone would help you win. Whether weak or strong you sing deep and you know your casements open on the view of a forlorn way the tower throws shadows to the far horizon to stop the music. Lucky for me that didn't stop you. But when will democracy arrive. You preach or sing. I don't see the cracks I have to find. You found the way, but with what discipline. I want to know how, but the music, the many instruments combining, all these nights of joy. It's what I wanted, everything we ever prayed for; and even so this music isn't quite enough to change the world. We let it be again. Oh my, it will be hard work to shift the paradigm. Begin at the beginning, the first thing to do is we look for the light, take chances. Here or in Manhattan. I've been there too. Then becomes now there if we betray ourselves. This time take Lufthansa's overnight flight to Berlin.

I passed through once by train, don't know anything first hand. You like it there I bet, and your audience loved you, you're in fashion always in Europe, it's less business than art, ain't that right mister. Here they understand what the I in your songs is saying. Don't they. Yet what they really like is your romantic aura, all these signs of wild living, even drugs perhaps, experience anyway, a luck that we (I'm there too) can't keep ourselves from envying. Even when you meditate, spiritual, or loving, a thin man in black you sing. I listen in the dark and don't mind. There is something to like in your strange integrity, it's what keeps us listening, reading. It happened that like some I came to you through books. That was my way; it still is. My sister heard you singing on her first record. I don't know why we gave it to her. But take it for what it's worth. Manhattan has the best record stores. Then it did anyway. But now we can buy your music anywhere, take your music. Even to Berlin.

And if only the books travelled as I do, that easily. How we would thank transnationals if only they cared for you enough to care for literacy too. For they own the airwaves and all those other technologies; so books are superfluous items in the global marketplace, even yours that dig deeper into the crack that you have always sung about casually. I sent for each book; they all sent me elsewhere, looking for cracks and light. The indeterminacy principle at work: I couldn't monkey with the universe while standing apart and observing it. It always gets away. The cracks are everywhere, jagged lightning on plywood like Paterson Ewen's. I listen to violin or saxophone when I write and I suspect you have; while the painter practiced listening to like sounds. I think every body dances to some music now. Night and day she stands before you and, amused and naked, waits for the now of eyes widening to the brightness. I'm here she says now are you ready. Down on your knees, that's the first gesture. Now look in the cracks. We have to do this together, let's take our time. You find them in Manhattan, in Montreal, even in that monastery. Then once more, over and over again we learn the first lesson: what to take with us, on our way to Berlin.

Remember, that's the key, you used to be me or somebody when you read or sang I understood you were talking to me. I used to believe in intimacy, something you gave to all of us, audience as I, to live in the light of song and changes. For better or worse, always the return of music, it changes it is the same. We remember performances, voices, and melodies to love. Oh, me? There are so many of us now. I and I once thought all your records brought something special to the ambient surround. Take your collage for Suzanne. I mean corsage. Arcane groceries float about our lady of the harbour. In one sense they always have. I think it's necessary to remember that too. All our father's gifts, our mother's nurturing inspire you. That day you drove all night listening to music and loving your friend forever then wrote down everybody's tender teenage dream that I won't be wounded by time like the others you're the first one ever to know this

16

that's what we read and heard. History teaches us to take the long view. By the waters of Manhattan you sat down and wept. To write then those Chelsea Hotel blues. No matter where we go, everywhere in the world, give or take a few small towns in Canada, is Berlin.

Soundcheck in Vienna, Austria, 1985
Photo by Michael Lohse

bill bissett

toasting   leonard   cohen   obviouslee

totalee xcellent   beautiful losers is wun uv
th greatest novels uv all time   so is th favorite
game   the book of mercy wun uv th greatest poetree
books uv all times as is   the energy of slaves

its closing time   is wun uv th greatest songs
uv all time   thees n all his othr works live
forevr in th heart   that still wants

happee birth day leonard cohen   love n rainbows
n magik lightning always   we ar all grateful

for yu   n love yu   thank yu   n love

GEORGE BOWERING

You'll Love It

Leonard Cohen keeps trying to do something he hasn't done before, and we find out again that he can do it. He can do it very well.

You want him to play some dinky little keyboard and sing along with the saxophone of Sonny Rollins? He'll do it.

Oh, I got the hots for Leonard Cohen, says some creature thirty years younger than me. Who the hell you talking about, I say.

Leonard, everyone loves or hates your novel—why don't you write another one, already? Guy hasn't read the novel.

God, look what he just did, says some reviewer, he's blown his reputation now, should have stuck with Phil Spector.

Millions of MTV fans, got their hats on backward, watch his video over and over, never read one of his poems. This matters?

I know a couple professors write serious books about Leonard Cohen and still like him. They found out they can do that more than once.

Suzanne takes you down with a step-over toe-hold. But can she pin you for the count of three?

Cohen's up. He's writing the libretto for a kind of opera you haven't even heard about yet, and I'll tell you something.

You'll hate it. It'll get better all the time. You'll love it.

ROBERT BRINGHURST

Bankei Yōkatu in Los Angeles

for Leonard Cohen

Light leaks from the mind like
tears from the eye,
blood from the body.

It flows from what-is like
sap from the tree. That is the only
reliable language.

What is is unborn.
Nevertheless,
it is already bearing.

The source of what was
is what is, and the source of what is
must be what will be.

What is is unborn.
What is born is a gesture
toward or away.

At the ends of the nerves,
what will be is breeding.
Being is bearing.

In bones and in river silt,
chromosomes, leaf-shapes,
in starlight and synapse and stone,

what no longer exists
is just shaving its face
and choosing its clothes.

What is is not yet born
and never will be,
yet these very words,

these very words
are listening
for all you have to say.

With good wishes to Leonard Cohen
on his 60th birthday

from the Editors and staff of

CANADIAN LITERATURE

W.H. New   E.-M. Kröller
Laurie Ricou   Beverly Westbrook

ADRIENNE CLARKSON

Leonard Cohen: A Monster of Love

Although I didn't meet Leonard until 1966, his words and imagination and poetic vision were with me for a long time, as with probably a number of young women who first read his slim volumes of poetry in the mid-Fifties. At the time, Canadian literature really didn't exist, but some of us became aware that two young men—one named Raymond Souster, and another Leonard Cohen, both from Montreal—were writing things that could really touch us. Apart from the fact that he mentioned places like Sherbrooke Street and snow, there was the throbbing romanticism of Leonard who, from his picture on the back of the cover, looked close enough to our age to make us throb as well.

And so it was that we tried to invite him to come to speak to us at St. Hilda's College (the Women's residence of the Anglican College at the University of Toronto, Trinity College). Somehow we couldn't get to him, and although we had so much wanted him to come to our monthly Literary Association meeting, it just didn't seem to work out. As Program Director for the Lit, as it was called, I had already committed to memory several of the poems, including the one with the lines "I heard of a man / who says words so beautifully / that if he only speaks their name / women give themselves to him." The idea that, in our English language and today in 1958, we could actually have someone who thought such things, much less wrote about them, was dizzying. I wanted him to come to our chaste residence and speak our names.

So I didn't meet Leonard Cohen in 1958, and my romances had to take other forms. I have often wondered what would have happened if he had come to us and brought us his unique visitation, not only of words but of spirit. Probably a couple of us wouldn't have lived our lives the way we decided to live them in the Sixties, and we might have learned to cultivate our deepest feelings and imagination in a more meaningful way than was

23

possible for proper, upper-middle-class girls of the late Fifties. He spoke to us; he kept us awake at night when we thought about his poetry. Unfortunately, he did not come to save us from middle-class ruin; we had to wait for his subtle undermining of our values in his songs.

So I was to wait until 1966, the first year I had a television programme and was interviewing full-time. This year coincided with the publication of Leonard's second novel, *Beautiful Losers*, which threw me into a complete daze. Its connection of the erotic with the prophetic was so astonishing that naturally it could not be understood in a purely Canadian context. This is a novel that requires the world as its audience, even though it is very particular in its detail about English- and French-Canadians and the first Native Canadian saint, Catherine Tekakwitha. It was two years before Pierre Elliot Trudeau startled us all into becoming our Prime Minister, but in some way it was part of the same *zeitgeist*, the same rush of intense emotion and meaning infusing public and private life, which we as Canadians have not known since. I believe that Leonard pre-figured this in literature and that in many ways Trudeau simply embodied what was already imaginatively real through Leonard's novel.

I remember the opening party given by the dynamic and committed Jack McClelland, at which everyone got ostentatiously drunk and said extravagant (and for Canada) daring things about the linking of sex and art. There for the first time I saw Leonard Cohen in the flesh: the dark eyes, the diffident manner and the sudden, childlike smile.

And then, just at the height of the reception of the novel, Leonard decided that he would not write poetry anymore but would become a singer. It was considered at the time to be risible. Many were the articles written that, although Leonard had no voice, he was going to attempt to be a singer. And thus it was that he appeared for the first time on television, singing on my CBC programme *Take 30*. He appeared with a small pop group called The Stormy Clovers, whose lead singer was an angelic blonde girl-child, herself the child of literati. Leonard appeared on the programme, and in dress rehearsal sang "Travel-

24

ler," which we timed out to be seventeen minutes long. The director, Cynthia Scott, came down to the floor to explain that we couldn't play a song that long (this was live television in those days) and Leonard, with the extreme politeness and sorrowful elegance which still marks his comportment, agreed to pull a verse. Also I remember he played "Suzanne" and "So Long Marianne." I of course was his undying fan and loved the tunes immediately. But there were grumbles elsewhere in the studio.

Interviewing him afterwards, I was so overcome by my admiration for him and by the years I had waited to meet him that it was not one of my finer moments professionally. I had reason to view the tape a few years ago, and thought myself ridiculous and my questions incredibly pompous. Or have styles changed since 1966? All I know is that I said to him rather portentously, "And so you now want to sing instead of write poetry?" The camera picked up his lambent eyes focusing on me mournfully as he answered, "Well, I think the time is over when poets should sit on marble stairs with black capes."

Years later I reminded him of this exchange and he laughed and said it was a toss-up as to which of us had been the more pompous. Happily, despite the fact of my inept questions and complete inability to deeply understand as opposed to react to his magical presence, we became friends of sorts. It is not a friendship of constant contact, but one that has seen all the years go by, and even with infrequent meetings, has had a deep and profound impact on me.

Although I really have to say it now: Leonard Cohen performs a priestly function. When I told him this once in Montreal, he took me to the entrance of the Jewish Cemetery at Outremont and showed me where his family are buried because they are Cohens, and of course Cohens are the hereditary priests of Israelites. I believe this to be the secret basis of his long-lasting appeal to two generations of people who love words and who can also laugh with them. Occasionally we have met in strange places—the Cafe Flore in Paris or on a street outside a sandwich shop in Toronto or once near 42nd Street in New York. Sometimes I wonder if Leonard was really there or if I wished him into being at those particular moments. It doesn't really matter. Magic is what he is.

And the magic he has summed up himself in *Beautiful Losers*:

> Something in him so loves the world that he gives himself to the laws of gravity and chance. Far from flying with the angels, he traces with the fidelity of a seismograph needle the state of the solid bloody landscape. His house is dangerous and finite, but he is at home in the world. He can love the shapes of human beings, the fine and twisted shapes of the heart. It is good to have among us such men, such balancing monsters of love. (*Beautiful Losers*, 1966, McClelland & Stewart Ltd., Toronto, p. 101)

ANDREI CODRESCU

for leonard cohen

the party was on the roof
of the chelsea hotel
above shelley winters' penthouse
a summer breeze started up
new york came to life in the evening
the girls began taking off their shirts
to dance
I was in heaven
I felt so glamorous
I was nineteen years old
and so was the world
I was but a year out of the old world
dressed in black from head to foot
still mourning sorrows I was beginning
to forget
the night was rose and soft
the girls were dancing bare-breasted
ah, what better place to be
a young poet in the late century
dancing with a sleepy-eyed beauty
with foam still clinging to her sea-fresh body
I closed my eyes

when I opened them
all the girls had vanished
I panicked
had the barbarians come
made off with the women?

no said someone
it was rumored that bob dylan
was visiting leonard cohen

in his room
and all the girls went there

the barbarians
were our heroes

In concert, 1973
Photographer unknown

JUDY COLLINS

Birthday Letter to Leonard

It was the fall of 1966, New York. I remember it well. I had not met you and I had not written a song of my own yet, although I was keeping journals already, some of them terribly dark. I lived on the upper west side of Manhattan and had been making records for six years, mostly the songs of city writers—Dylan-Seeger-Malvina Reynolds—and haunting melodies from antiquity. I searched for writers unknown and songs that were timeless.

I had been sick with hepatitis and, as I recovered, I did a lot of thinking about directions in my music. I knew I was at a point of transformation in my music, metamorphosis. I could feel it coming.

While you were writing poems and books and songs in Montreal that summer, I memorized Brecht and sang Beatles songs, went to see Peter Brook's "Marat / Sade" and was so taken with Richard Peaslee's music, I put the score on tape and edited it to hear what it might sound like. I planned the new album. "In My Life" was going to be something theatrical, something different, I began to play the piano again. The scales and Czerny and Hanon filled the apartment, all those years of Mozart came flooding back.

My friend Mary Martin told me about a man in Montreal. "Poet," she said, "novelist, his name is Leonard Cohen. He's written some songs, and I like them a lot," she said. "And I think you should hear them."

You came down from Montreal on a Thursday according to my diary. We talked that night, Earl Robinson was visiting and we went out to dinner with Earl and some other friends, and you were charming, easy, very striking looking and you did not sing that night. I think you were living at the Chelsea Hotel then. I remember I wasn't drinking.

The next night you came back and sang me two songs—"Dress Rehearsal Rag" and "Suzanne." I was amazed and changed by these songs. It was as though I had ordered them up and some mystic muse had brought them, with your voice, your lyric, your music.

I recorded both songs, and convinced you to sing at the benefit at Town Hall in New York that winter. You were a new face, a new name, and I think my record of your songs had just been released. You came out on the stage with your guitar and began to sing "Suzanne," and then froze mid-verse, petrified, and walked off the stage.

I think of that as one of your finest moments. Because you came back. And kept coming back. You went on to become one of the most magnificent performers I have ever heard.

One of the books that has most affected me is Flannery O'Connor's collection of letters, *The Habit of Art*. You have a habit of art, you move me with all your songs, whether I record them or not.

"Sisters of Mercy" always reminds me of that time in Newport when I had arranged the first singer-songwriter afternoon with you and Joni Mitchell and Mike Settle and Janis Ian. And that young man named Douglas who slept with me in the same room where you were busy writing in your diary, or perhaps writing "The Future." You Inspire Trust.

"Joan of Arc" has come back to me again recently in another incarnation, speaking to me of the elements; earth, fire, water, stone, fragility and power that speak through your lyrics. I still sing "Bird on the Wire," which I think of as a blues. I don't sing many blues. I live the blues, but you write the blues I can sing.

I eat the black Abaddo dates you sent me for Christmas and go over the list again—"Priests," "Hey, That's No Way to Say Goodbye," "Story of Isaac," "Blue Raincoat," "Bernadette" which I will record someday but haven't yet. So many songs. In all I have recorded a dozen.

Since this is your birthday, I would like to give you a gift of gratitude, a present, as you have been present in my psyche for all these years. I remember years before I heard "The Future" that night at a party when you took me aside from the swirl of guests and bullshit, off to a corner where you told me all the lyrics of "Democracy."

But the gratitude I extend to you can not be thanks for your even more real and true gift to me.

You were the one who told me to write songs.

You said "If I can do it," braving the stage at Town Hall, petrified, singing "Suzanne," "you can do it."

And so I took my dark journals, my threads and wisps of poetry in search of life, of melody, and I risked the leap you didn't say would be safe, into the arms of my own muse.

She is different from your muse, of course. And she has tantrums and walks out of the room after an argument, but I think she's getting kinder. Or maybe tougher. She doesn't drink. And sometimes I imagine our muses are at least sisters in some ether in the other plane in which they dwell with all the other muses who live and breathe, mustering the force to fill our hearts with fire. Like "Sisters of Mercy."

When I sing my songs—"Since You've Asked," "My Father," "Houses," "The Blizzard"—they reverberate with that enchanted gift you were the first to give.

On your sixtieth birthday, know that you have been an ageless inspiration to me. I sing your beautiful, moving, timeless and transformational songs.

And I sing my own songs. That is your gift to me.

Happy Birthday, dear Leonard.

JOHN ROBERT COLOMBO

A Question for a Poet

There is a question I would like to ask Leonard Cohen. I would ask it but for the fact that he might even answer it. And I am not sure I ever want to learn the answer!

It is all rather involved, so I have to tell a little story. Here goes . . .

It was a dark and stormy night. It actually *was* a dark and stormy night, in Toronto, about 1965. My wife Ruth and I were among a handful of guests at a gathering at the home on Inglewood Drive of Elizabeth and Jack McClelland. It was an impromptu gathering of some authors and editors connected with the McClelland and Stewart publishing company.

Among the guests were the novelist Scott Symons (we were meeting for the first time) and Leonard Cohen (we kept encountering each other . . . once, two years earlier, with Irving Layton, in my own living room!).

Leonard may not have been the recording artist that he later became, but even then he was someone special. His prose and poetry had its own appeal and style, and he radiated a peculiar charisma. He was a legend in his golden youth, a prophet with honour in his own country.

The gathering broke up about half an hour after midnight. Ruth and I were standing in the McClelland hallway when it occurred to me to offer drives to those with no cars. It was drizzling and no taxis were in evidence. Scott readily accepted the offer; so did Leonard.

As I recall, Scott was staying in Riverdale, somewhere east of the Don River, so we drove there first and dropped him off. Leonard was next. He said he was staying for a few days in a small hotel in downtown Toronto, located a few miles to the west.

The route took us through a rough section of the city, a section with more than the usual share of dilapidated billboards, silent factories, railway tracks, cracked sidewalks, weeds and indus-

32

trial waste. No one was on the streets; even vehicular traffic was limited. Bursts of light came from the twin headlights of the occasional truck or taxi. Through the drizzle and the action of the windshield wipers, the dreary sight resembled the scene in a spy movie with bleary chase sequences through an abandoned factory district in a city somewhere in Eastern Europe in the depths of the Cold War.

I would have driven faster but the road was slippery and irregular and caution prevailed. Conversation in the car was warm and animated. I seem to remember we were discussing Irving Layton and his passionate poems. Suddenly Leonard said, "I'll get out here."

"Pardon?" I asked.

"I'll leave here, if you'll stop."

I slowed down.

"You want to get out here, in the rain?" I asked, surprised.

"Yes."

I stopped. Through the streaky windows of the car I surveyed the scene to discern what it was that Leonard had seen that I had not noticed.

There was nothing at all that was inviting or intriguing. No people, no bar, no greasy spoon, no cornerstore, no fine and private place, no vista, no bright streetlight, no waiting taxi. It was a desolate scene.

Yet for the first time it occurred to me that the scene was not without the poetry of life. Although it was as dispiriting a sight short of suffering that any number of big cities could offer, the setting was still a human creation. It had its emotion. The ambience was yet alive. I sensed that this was what appealed to Leonard. Maybe I was right, maybe wrong. Perhaps there was something else.

I sought confirmation. "You're sure you don't want us to drive you back to the hotel to pick up your raincoat and then bring you back here."

"No."

In a low voice, tendering his thanks, Leonard slipped out the car door into the wet of the night. As we drove away, I watched his figure diminish in the distance until it disappeared among the shadows of the factories.

A few blocks later I said to Ruth, "I wonder if there'll be a news item in the newspaper tomorrow afternoon with the heading MONTREAL POET DISAPPEARS IN TORONTO."

No such headline appeared the next day, nor the day after. Leonard did not disappear, at least on that occasion. Instead, he turns up repeatedly in Montreal and Los Angeles, in Toronto and Vienna. . . .

But to this day I find myself pondering the incident and posing the following question: "Leonard, what did you find when you slipped out of the car on that dark and stormy night in Toronto?"

LORNA CROZIER

I Know I'm Not Supposed To Say It, But

I miss the smokers, the heavy drinkers
though my eyes burn when someone lights
a cigarette. I miss the poet who drank
a bottle of gin a day and talked to his
parrot in bird-vowels of squeaks and squawks,
its eyes following his big gentle hands
stumbling through the air. I miss the post-coital
smoke of my lover as he raised two fingers
that smelled of me to his mouth and inhaled
again and again. I miss the whiskey priest who danced
wet in his robes in the fountain below the Spanish Steps,
holding a gelato high above his head and
never dropping it. I miss the tin tobacco can
of my 60-cigarette-a-day mother-in-law who insisted
she didn't inhale. I miss my father who asked me
to smuggle a case of beer into the cancer ward,
who dragged his intravenous stand to the dungeon
smoking room whenever someone came to visit.
I miss the artist in Zagreb who for over an hour
in the bar tried to touch the mole on my shoulder
and always overshot his mark, his yellow-stained
finger jabbing the air. I miss the beautiful
woman who drank scotch with Dylan Thomas. After three
scotch on ice, she tossed her head all night,
throwing back the long hair she didn't have anymore.
I miss the smokers, the heavy drinkers,
the ones who walked naked through parties,
covered with the host's shaving cream, the ones
who pushed dill pickles into their ears,
who played the harmonica with their noses,
who could aim a smoke ring to settle like a halo
over someone's blessed head. I miss them on the couch

where I covered them with the extra blanket,
where I took the glowing ember from between their fingers.
I miss climbing the stairs to bed, draped in their silky
cape of smoke, their singing and jubilation, the small
bonfires of their bodies burning through
what little was left of the night.

Backstage in Vienna, 1988
Photo by Michael Lohse

CHARLIE DANIELS

For Leonard

I met Leonard in the late sixties when he came to Nashville to record his *Songs from a Room* album.

I was a bluegrass rock and roller, fresh from the rowdy smoke-filled barrooms of America. A string-stretching, stage-stomping rebel, with my head in the clouds and my amplifier on ten.

To say that I was an unlikely candidate to be a part of Leonard's music would be a gross understatement.

His songs were sensitive and fragile, his style soft and moody, his imagery deep and thought provoking, and his music foreign to a kid from North Carolina, who cut his teeth on Elvis and had electricity in his blood.

Leonard Cohen opened up a whole new world of music for me.

He took me to Paris and London, to the concert stages of the world.

I sat behind him, thrilling to the soft acoustical sounds that we were playing for the crowds, who sat in rapt and respectful silence.

I developed a great respect for his poetry and music and in the process learned to love the man. I still do.

Happy birthday, old friend.

BEA DE KONING & YVONNE HAKZE

On his 60th birthday we would like to thank Leonard for:

•The Songs — Ever since I was 16 and I heard "Suzanne" for the first time, the songs have been part of my life. Even now when I hear a Cohen song on the radio in the morning, it makes my day. It's like meeting an old friend unexpectedly. I remember sitting in the hallway of a hospital waiting for the doctor, when suddenly somewhere far away, somebody opened a door and I heard Leonard singing "So Long, Marianne," and I knew that the doctor had good news for me. When I hear "First We Take Manhattan" in the supermarket, I forget what I have to buy and just listen to the music.

• The Poems — After listening to "Suzanne" for the first time, I wanted to know more about this singer, this man. I discovered that he wrote books and poems. For my birthday, my brother gave me *The Spice Box of Earth*, and I fell in love with poetry. Maybe I would have found my way to poetry eventually, but it was Leonard who opened that door for me.

• The Friends — When Yvonne and I started *Intensity*, it was just a small Dutch magazine, just to keep in touch with the other Cohen fans in the country. But somehow, Cohen fans from all over the world got in touch with us. Wherever we travel throughout the world—Ireland, Germany, the USA, Canada—there are always friends to stay with. When you visit them, you feel immediately at home. They have the same record collection as you, and their bookcase looks like the one you have at home. You have much more in common than just Cohen's songs—even their refrigerator door looks like yours (a Cohen picture).

If someone gives you all that, there is a lot to be thankful for. We would like to thank Leonard for all that and wish him many more productive years.

JIM DEVLIN

After all these years, I can't remember the chap's exact words, but it was something like: ". . . Ladies and Gentlemen, we regret that the Leonard Cohen concert will not be starting on time as there are still a few problems with the sound . . . we hope it will not be too long before the start of the concert and we do apologise for this delay . . . " The P.A. clicked off.

Some of us just shrugged, lots made a low, groaning noise (not quite in harmony but it suggested E minor to me), and others continued to pore eagerly through Leonard's new book, *Death of a Lady's Man*. I'd just bought my copy that night too, and inscribed it immediately—London, December 4, 1979, Hammersmith Odeon.

After about twenty minutes, a few fans started singing 'Why are we waiting?', taken up good humouredly by quite a few more (perhaps now in G minor) and any tension among the waiting throng was easily dissolved. *Everyone* found their voice at about 8:30 and united in a great cheer when the doors finally opened and we flooded in for the concert.

And what a concert! I didn't have a pen or pencil to jot down the songs (my first regret of the evening, though only a slight one); in hindsight, mind you, after the first few songs, I'd probably not have been able to do so as Leonard was slowly and inexorably weaving his magic web of sound throughout the auditorium, wrapping us all in his famous blue raincoat, demanding our silence at the trial of a singer who had to die, begging us to tell him the whereabouts of his gypsy wife . . . He sang and sang and sang. His voice and guitar and back-up musicians (a young 'fusion' band to quote the programme, called Passenger, plus violinist Raffi Hakopian and several others) filled the place with so many of his familiar and best-loved songs in such fresh arrangements they (almost) sounded like new songs; and even those from his most recent album—*Recent Songs*, of course (which

40

I played over and over again since its release a couple of months earlier)—sounded new and a little unfamiliar. Perhaps it was just the excitement of being at my first Leonard Cohen concert; perhaps because it was my first ever gig at the Hammersmith Odeon; or maybe, and perhaps *this* is the real reason: it was just . . . the songs. Sung by their best singer, their composer.

Leonard was dressed in black; and when singing solo, standing in the spotlight, he delivered his lines with emotion, passion and verve; and in one particular song, "Memories", with a great sense of humour—complete with "Sha la la's" and dancing girls—Jennifer Warnes and Sharon Robinson, his brilliant back-up vocalists, doing a marvellous Ronettes routine! God, it made me laugh; and not only me, for the whole place echoed with cheers and laughter every time he belted out

"Ah but won't you let me see
I said won't you let me see
Won't you let me seeeeeeeeeeeee
Your naked body?
Aaaaaaaaaaaahhhhhh aaaaahhhhhhh"

Of course we had the *real* Cohen too; lovely versions of "Who by Fire", "Chelsea Hotel #2", "Field Commander Cohen", and many more. Sometimes a song-title was shouted out from the audience but from where I was sitting I couldn't tell if Leonard obliged—he just kept singing one great song after another.

I had to leave before the end (obviously my biggest regret of the evening) to catch a midnight train; but I carried away with me my own set of memories which have lasted ever since. This Leonard Cohen concert which for me had promised so much, had, in truth, delivered so much much more.

ANN DIAMOND

Losers, Sore and Beautiful

I would like to confess that Cohen's *Beautiful Losers* (first published in 1966) remains the Canadian novel to which I compare most others. Mind you, I also love Hugh MacLennan's *The Watch That Ends the Night*, but *Beautiful Losers* coincided with my coming of age. What still most impresses me is its treatment of Canadian history. Cohen tells it from the losers's point of view: that of the Indians and the French. Being a Jew led him to identify with the victims, and to fashion a compellingly spiritual interpretation of the drama called Canada: one that didn't politely leave out sex or race, but wove them into the fabric of our sometimes-suicidal, sometimes-murderous striving to exist here.

When it came out, of course, it was generally reviled by Canadian critics, and even provoked a little anti-semitic mail. Many considered it inferior to his first novel, *The Favorite Game,* but in recent years the post-modern crowd have decided that *Beautiful Losers* was a kind of forerunner of *their* work. Unfortunately, few of them can match the all-out passion of its style or equal its depth of vision.

Beautfiul Losers gave free verbal rein to historical agony, which doesn't make it any less hilarious. Cohen based much of it on the Jesuit Records whose pious accounts of religious conversions were interspersed with hallucinatory notes describing demons and celestial signs: testimony to the severe culture shock that missionaries often felt in bringing their faith to a hostile wilderness.

Recently I read that great catastrophist, Emmanuel Velikovsky, on the human capacity for forgetting nasty experiences. Remember the last time our planet was knocked off course by an asteroid? Of course you don't, silly—you've *repressed it*! Strategic amnesia also applies in literature. The destinies of writers revolve a bit like planets, sometimes shining brilliantly, sometimes going into eclipse as their ideas wander in and out of vogue.

It reminds me that good fiction is closely tied to history, and to what Freud calls "repetition compulsion." Artists are often driven by a compulsion to repeat—symbolically and (usually) harmlessly—past traumas which would otherwise fall into the unconscious and cause damage. What I call good fiction is a wholehearted reliving of the real chaos and horror that—let's face it—underlie most of history's great events. Out of every glorious victory comes scores of walking wounded, the Beautiful or just Sore Losers whose voices are often heard only in great art.

Bad fiction, a.k.a. literary kitsch, stems from the opposite tendency: a desire to repress historical trauma. "Let's not go into it" is its motto. Much of our mainstream culture follows this dictum. After a working vacation in the birthplace of tragedy, I find Canadians look more than ever like a nation of dolled-up sublimators, frozen in postures of polite denial. Perhaps this is the price our writers pay for recognition.

Even our own (reconsidered) Leonard Cohen, once the Prince of Catharsis, whose early song lyrics still roar like a motorcade from Hell, can now face the nation on the Ralph Benmergui show and spell out his new motto: "Mum's the word."

Whose word? Whose Mum?

The one who always told us there'd be days like this?

MARY DI MICHELE

A Bouquet of Rapini

Eating is touch carried to the bitter end.

I'll be there today with a big bouquet of cactus.
I got this rig that runs on memory.
                                        —Leonard Cohen

                    1

The vegetable is bitter green
                        and full of *vita*
amens, the iron i
                need, my blood
tired from a whole
                    lotta loveless
        ness and it's nicely
                            wrapped as if it were a gift
and it is
            my trophy, it has real weight

this bouquet, but the
                    man, the wished for

end to a long line of men
offers me something fresh, something nurturing
he fills me up with much more than the daily
recommended ferrous sulphate and folic acid

                    2

You know romance is roses
but the pattern on the paper is not
                            what's inside

44

3

No, it's not
        flowers he brings
what i need
        his body, his bloody
                rapini, its scent of rain in tin

cans is better for my health and he's so
good to me i'm surprised when he won't
stay to dine because his taste is for
alone, doesn't need my love, just breathing

                        room

                          and the men

4

u's planned for one perhaps
                he's gone
for good this time
                O woman starved
O woman buy your own
                rapini for $2.50 a small bunch
at le Fauborg. No price
is too high. Thanks to him

i've become good at cooking
myself.

5

Steam rapini or drop into a few inches of salted, rapidly boiling
water until tender, they turn bright green. They look more alive
when cooked like lobster. Their stillness seems contemplative.

45

Heat olive oil, extra
virgin in a frying pan. Sliver cloves of garlic,
many, and cook until golden along with some red dried chili
peppers. Drop the steamed rapini into the oil and stir fry. May be
served as a side dish or on top of pasta along with some ricotta
cheese you simply warm in the pan with the rapini for one
minute or two.

6

        at pumping irony.
Away from him this strength is new, is
            nautilus, i lie
alone in bed and like it
observe these arms are winter
        white and the bicep
muscle is taut, is long
        lean and feline, the lynx,

7

before it devours the inner child
        as it crouches to spring
or before it settles to sleep
        curled under the snow.

BARBARA DODGE

Sonnet for Leonard

I met Leonard in 1970 at our favorite bar in Montreal called The Winston Churchill Pub. He had just returned from New York and invited me to join him for dinner at The Pantheon, a famous Montreal Greek restaurant. During the course of a fabulous dinner, he presented me with the Greek evil eye, to "protect my virginity" he said.

I am happy to report that it only protected my virginity with him. And I'm probably the only one who was able to resist this woman's man. I have never known a more seductive, compelling Lothario. And, in Montreal, Leonard was our man, the voice that gave dimension and colour to the boites and cobbled streets and dim, Napoleonic dreams of a forgotten, misidentified culture in a way no one before or since him has.

He is an astounding novelist, poet, songwriter. Leonard, I celebrate with you this tribute . . . and I send this sonnet with my heartfelt gratitude for your contribution to all of our memories.

Your longing songs have given me the rise
Remembrance brings, escaping sorrow's gift
The slain have not forgotten, nor what's left
Of neighbourhood's remains, the withered rose
Some love disdains which time's discarded face
Retains like warrant of each newborn wave.
You went away, in silence, to believe
Your songs that sing without you could replace
Your longing satisfied with longing we
Deceive; and I have loved you long who sang
This song familiarly, where flowers mourn
The winter's day that takes their bright glory
Crying from our clay, where you went kneeling
Through the dark, and I watched you all alone.

STAN DRAGLAND

F. ing Through *Beautiful Losers*

Not all readers in the free love sixties and early seventies could stand the kinky sex in *Beautiful Losers,* and I doubt that those few among the shocked who hung on long enough to realize what the sex was doing in the novel ("Hard cock alone leads to Thee") would have been reassured. Sex was not the only obstacle, when there was one. I remember people who should have known better feeding the rumour that *Beautiful Losers* had been a perfectly good straightforward novel until Cohen got on drugs and scrambled the damn thing. Not everyone was a convert, then, but *Beautiful Losers* was a holy book for many readers of the Age of Aquarius who simply inhaled it, as uncritically as those novel readers of Henry James's age who had the "comfortable, goodhumoured feeling . . . that a novel is a novel, as a pudding is a pudding, and that our only business with it could be to swallow it" (165).

For me, at first, Cohen's novel didn't go down so easily. It was the first weird book I'd ever read. There wasn't much context for it in the Canada of 1966, not that I knew of anyway, nothing like the postmodernism of writers like Ondaatje and Bowering who owe something to *Beautiful Losers* and haven't forgotten that. Certainly no criticism like Linda Hutcheon's *The Canadian Postmodern,* which begins with *Beautiful Losers.* I made no connection between Cohen's experimentation and that of writers elsewhere. The most unusual other book I had read by then was *Ulysses,* and this was so literary as to feel familiar enough. Coming to *Beautiful Losers* cold (except for scarcely believable reports of Cohen's reading from it at The University of Alberta - "slof tlif, sounded the geysers of his semen as they hit the dashboard"— and Desmond Pacey's appearance there to declare it a masterpiece!), it might have stumped me had I not been a more talented reader then than I am now. Then I read like an antelope grafted to a steamroller: I could leap the incomprehensible and flatten the complex. So I could jump from section to section, book to book, absorbed mainly by the chronological story of Catherine Tekakwitha. She was historical and thus "real." "This material has a power of its own, doesn't it" (212), says F. while he is finishing the story of Catherine (become a sort of collaborative hagiography) that his friend began. That's how *I* felt, and I still do. As Catherine is transformed into an Iroquois virgin, her uncle realizes that "Our heaven is dying" (94); the Christians are going to win. Catherine's achievement is a poignant anomaly in a religious tragedy which moved me.

But I wasn't paying much attention to wild cards: this material is actually joked through, annotated and infiltrated by anachronism, generally shunted around by narrators who have several additional matters on their minds. And the comprehensible seventeenth century plot begins inside a present-day fiction, the story of an unnamed narrator, a scholar, desperately courting the Indian Virgin with his words for solace from continuous grief, whose narrative is all over the place, as you might expect from a man whose "Brain Feels Like It Has Been Whipped" (58). "Cohen keeps about twelve incidents going at the same time," says Michael Ondaatje (*Leonard Cohen* 49), one of the reasons why Ondaatje's *Coming Through Slaughter* has haunted my recent reading of *Beautiful Losers*. In Buddy Bolden's music, "He would be describing something in 27 ways" (37).

The context of Canadian postmodernist fiction slowly grew up around *Beautiful Losers,* helping to make its discontinuities legible. But the first stage of critical response, when receptive, sifted and sorted through the novel under the influence of practical criticism, with its assumption of a text's underlying unity. Stephen Scobie's book on Cohen performs a sophisticated version of my leaping steamroller, offering a detailed chart of the novel, with everything joined to everything else, each motif pattern rendered about as significant as any other. Scobie wouldn't do that now. At least his (to use Rafael Barreto-Rivera's pun in *Nimrod's Tongue* 27) Derridative treatment of *Death of a Lady's Man* in *Signature Event Cantext* suggests that he too is not the reader he was.

49

My own first critical approach to *Beautiful Losers,* mercifully hidden in old lecture notes, was also bent to show how the novel made sense. For students, good inhalers short on analytic skills, this was maybe a service. But I see now how limiting it was. Especially I see how much my approach depended on a selective reading of the character of F. It was and is much easier for the reader to become a student of F.—to swallow his teachings as though his authority were not immediately limited by his fictionality—than it is for the reluctant disciple/narrator of Book I, suffering his bereavements and the apparent waste of his life. The reader, re-reading, may study at leisure the pronouncement of a guru reduced to the black of words on a white page.

The words are flesh to the narrator of Book One, "The History of Them All," much of which is a howl not only of pain but of bewilderment because he was/is the reluctant disciple of a teacher whose classroom is hysteria (59) whose teachings are at once persuasive and incomprehensible. "Mindfucks," Dennis Lee calls them in *Savage Fields* (69). It's one thing to see as through a glass, darkly, and it's another to have to try to see as through a prism of funhouse mirrors, through F., best friend since orphanage days, charismatic charlatan. His rendition of the Platters' "The Great Pretender" is probably not merely a love lament. "Take one step to the side and it's all absurd" (37), the narrator realizes. What is it that tempts me (being, in my relationship to *Beautiful Losers,* something like this man to F.) not to take that side-step? F.'s "system," his outrageous salad of world myths and religions tossed with contemporary advertising, movies, porn, comics, cartoons, the Top Forty, you name it—all of it accepted as sacred material—is couched in such passionate rhetoric and poetry that it's almost possible to give in to it. The fascination of F., this desire to believe what he says, is astonishing, provoked as it is by a novel so little bound by the conventions of realism. The stakes are high, of course. If F. were real and if he knew what he was talking about (forgetting for the moment the cracks in his consistency, forgetting that he's made of words), then everything in the modern world would make sense, the whole painful puzzle would be whole, as it once was, in "an eternal eye" (17), just as bracingly difficult of approach as ever. Any amount of suffering could be endured. Like the narrator of Borges' "The Library of Babel," crying the frustration of his search for so much as an inkling of meaning in his labyrinthine universe/library, many are lonely for the lack of such belief:

> If honor and wisdom and happiness are not for me, let them be for others. Let heaven exist, though my place be in hell. Let me be outraged and annihilated, but for one instant, in one being, let Your enormous library be justified" (*Labyrinths* 57).

Yes, F. is seductive; his system has its attractions. But not, I expect, when all things are considered, to the squeamish. A reader who listens to everything F. says, the depressive lapses in confidence as well as the manic persuasiveness, is going to draw away from him. A reader who ponders *all* the words, even the puzzling ones, in the system—the novel—that contains F., finds it quite like F.'s character at face value, inconsistent and undependable. Like looking at the northern lights when the spirits are particularly active: the whole design pulses to some configuring energy, but centre and all are constantly shifting. In fiction, isn't continual change more exhilarating to a reader (especially when she joins the process) than the centre holding (still)? If we stop expecting sense to be made in the old ways, it is. Form and chaos cohabit everywhere.

Reading all the words, trying to stay free. As a child I was the antelope, reading voraciously with a naive sort of rigour only the words that interested me. Never contemplating response in any making of my own whether creative or critical. This much of that illusory freedom I wish to keep in these latter days: to honour theory in my writing only where it's wild, lifting hot off the critical occasions it collects and baptises reluctantly; theory in the bone. "Play with me, old friend" (159), F. says posthumously to his disciple. Join in, he means (to slide over the sexual connotation), go with it. Life is [*Beautiful Losers* is] a fabulous game with fluid rules and no possibility of winning.

But F. can't sustain his belief, if belief it is and not "a mood

51

gone absolute" (Lee, *Civil Elegies* 55). Suffering and doubt is all the narrator of Book One possesses, so he thinks. He has no system, no theory. Sometimes he sees that F. suffers, but he doesn't seek an outlet from his own pain by reinterpreting F. in that light. To a reader standing somewhere between the two, a lot of what F. says comes to sound like bravado. "Oh, F." asks the disciple of his master, "do you think I can learn to perceive the diamonds of good amongst all the shit?" "It is all diamond, " F. replies, characteristically (9). Easy for *him* to say?

One way to read *Beautiful Losers* is as a journey—of the narrator, of Catherine, gathering other selves as they go—through the shit to the diamond. Another approach, unlinear, is suggested by the fact that the pain and the questions don't disappear, the shit doesn't go away. Neither is absent from the novel's ending(s), spoken by some survivor with a breaking heart. In Michael Ondaatje's rewriting of F., "The diamond had to love the earth it passed along the way, every speck and angle of the other's history, for the diamond had been earth too" (111).

*

Not all sections of Book One advance the plot. Eight of them are tours de force with a rhetoric and a structure of their own, several others have large set-pieces embedded in them, and the text lurches or slides into a virtual anthology of briefer set pieces. There is, in general, such volatility of voice, such thoroughly polyphonic notation of the sounds of "the tinkly present" (75) that one might be reminded—of the dolphin sonographs (depicting multiple simultaneous vocalizations) in the epigraph to Ondaatje's *Slaughter* (6). Yes, but I was thinking of Cohen's bird: "Experts with tape recorders say that what we hear as a single bird note is really ten or twelve tones with which the animal weaves many various beautiful liquid harmonies" (117). Catbird, maybe: one of the avian parodists capable of alternating the dulcet with the dissonant.

Few sections of Book One are stylistically "pure," and few readers have made much of this pyrotechnique. Not surprisingly, Michael Ondaatje is an exception. He sees "the essential drama of the novel in the styles Cohen uses" (*Leonard Cohen* 47), and he reflects the critical consensus that the variety of Book One illustrates the narrator's failure to fit things together. It is true that his lonely limited first-person world must collapse before something familial and ecstatic may reassemble from the fragments (this is in F.'s syllabus) but we need also to consider the *behaviour* of this man's words. A character who can raise his normal colloquial style into elegant prose and also sink into gibberish or virtually speak in tongues is protean, and hardly the sad useless dead-end dummy he thinks he is. It doesn't even matter if his style has been "colonized" by the extravagant F., that much of his style and substance doesn't belong to him, to either of them. In this he is like people in general—derivative, "intertextual"—only more and more obviously so.

Book One's narrator is abulge with the babel of the world. He is too many for us. He spills over the edges of system. He enacts a freedom that is unfortunately no bloody good to him; hence the torment in so much of *what* he says. Like all the best clowns he is often hilarious with his breaking heart on his sleeve. To enjoy his Book Three performance of a "remote human possibility" (101), a miracle, it helps to realize that the narrator of Book One *is* his style—as long as we're seeing him as a character in the conventional sense. In another perspective he is an ego too beautifully de-centered to be able to absorb and dissolve the traces of his culture that stream through him. They leave his style striated with their own signatures.

Book Two is "A Long Letter from F.," epistolary in form and pedagogical in intent. F. now exposes his aims and his method, sure that his pupil knows all that losing his mind can teach him. An irony retroactively spreads over Book One when F. reveals that he is only "the Moses of our little exodus. I would never cross" (178). "Go forth," F. says, "teach the world what I meant to be" (169). "I wanted to be a magician," he goes on, in a more generic metaphor, "That was my idea of glory. Here is a plea based on my whole experience: do not be a magician, be magic" (175). If the man with the system is merely the forerunner, we need to reconsider the value (without forgetting the pain) of the one who loses control.

Book Two is more continuous and stylistically less varied than Book One, though certainly not uniform. In his narrative of Catherine's last four years, F's style carries marks of his friend's style, with Jesuit originals and other source-styles layered in, but even in his letter proper he bursts into a poem, "God is Alive, Magic is Afoot," and inserts three quatrains of unattributed poetry (the same poem; different ones?) into the Argentine Hotel scene. And the novel's total anthology of styles is swollen by the catalogues, blurbs and samples of material generated by the pornography and sex aids industry that F. reads in the attempt to stimulate Edith to orgasm. Not even a recitation of the martyrdom of Brebeuf will work, however—and that extreme incongruity gives a clue why *Beautiful Losers* fails utterly as pornography: those not offended or simply aghast are more likely to be startled into laughter than aroused.

Between that epic sex scene and the sequel of Catherine's story two poems appear: a sonnet called "F.'s Invocation to History in the Old Style," and a quatrain entitled "F.'s Invocation to History in the Middle Style." The first could conceivably be read as a symbolic condensation of the whole novel, including Book Three ("I see an Orphan, lawless and serene, / standing in a corner of the sky" 200-201); the second is (very characteristic of F.) nonsense, "drug addict's argot" (201) compacted to meaninglessness and the joke extended by seven explanatory footnotes, with notes on the footnotes infiltrated by extensions of F.'s letter to his friend. F.'s photographic memory will have retained his friend's scholarly method as one more style to parody.

F. takes some pains with the remainder of Catherine's tale, which may seem inconsistent with advising his friend to "Read it with that part of your mind which you delegate to watching out for blackflies and mosquitoes" (200). Is he still giving with one hand and taking away with the other? Maybe not. He wants the mind's watchdogs drugged so there's no filter of the real. You see clearly only out of the corner of your eye. Anyway, the continuation of Catherine's tale is hardly that only. F.'s letter contin-

54

ues to flow through it, as F. explicitly draws the parallels between Edith's life and Catherine's. He almost imperceptibly shifts the setting to that of the final scene of the epilogue, as well. "We are now in the heart of the winter of 1680," says F., as he begins, "We are now in the heart of our pain. We are now in the heart of our evidence" (218). Who is "we"? F. and Edith and her husband and probably you and I and the author, the whole ensemble beginning to roll together towards the epilogue, as the "we are now" motif survives the end of Catherine's story: "We are now in the heart of the System Theatre," "We are now in the heart of the last feature in the System Theatre" (235-236). We are travelling forward to hook the events of the Epilogue to the end of Book One, and back into F.'s memory of himself and his two friends watching a movie, to the moment when his own attention is distracted to the projected ray itself.

In another refrain that links his letter and his narrative of Catherine, F. has been showing his friend "how it happens." Some variation on this phrase occurs several times. In fact the active presentness of both refrains chimes with the spirit of beginnings invoked in Section 21, which is out in left field, having nothing to do with Catherine:

> Like a numbered immigrant in the harbor of North America, I hope to begin again. I hope to begin my friendship again. I hope to begin my rise to President. I hope to begin Mary again. I hope to begin my worship again to Thee who has never refused my service, in whose flashing memory I have no past or future, whose memory never froze into the coffin of history . . . (228).

(I can't let this passage slip by without remarking slight turbulences in it: the myth of America as promised land of equal opportunity is a banal Norman Rockwell vision elsewhere in the novel; and who is "Thee"? The answer would seem obvious if the flashing and the collapsing of time weren't so reminiscent of the transformed narrator in the Epilogue.)

Just before the last scene in which F. is given up to the dogs he presents the question he claims tormented him during the silvery hours he and his two friends spent at the System Theatre (an appropriately named but nevertheless actual Montreal cinema): *"What will happen when the newsreel escapes into the Feature?"*

> The newsreel lies between the street and the Feature like Boulder Dam, vital as a border in the Middle East —breach it (so I thought), and a miasmal mixture will imperialize existence by means of its sole quality of total corrosion. (so I thought) The newsreel lies between the street and the Feature: like a tunnel on the Sunday drive it ends quickly and in creepy darkness joins the rural mountains to the slums. It took courage! I let the newsreel escape, I invited it to walk right into plot, and they merged in aweful originality, just as trees and plastic synthesize new powerful landscapes in those districts of the highway devoted to motels. Long live motels, the name, the motive, the success! Here is my message, old lover of my heart. Here is what I saw: here is what I learned:
> Sophia Loren Strips For A Flood Victim
> THE FLOOD IS REAL AT LAST (237-238)

This is the second epitome of F.'s system, "God is Alive" being the first. He seems to have forgotten having already summed everything up. It's good that F.'s old lover has been prepared to receive this new message (so might run a reader's first reaction), because it makes no sense to me. But the reader has also been learning, or should have been; we are reading F.'s letter over the shoulder of a man whose cluelessness (his own Book One contains a very high proportion of questions) is not foreign to us. Well *have* we been learning? Here is the relevant lesson: "To understand the truth in anything that is alien, first dispense with the indispensable in your own vision" (89). No sooner heard than accepted. On to Book Three.

Just kidding.

The newsreel is both a border and a tunnel, fencing out the Feature and also connecting with it, but underground, not obviously. My paraphrase turns simile into metaphor and conceals my guesswork. Nowadays the newsreel has been dignified with the name of documentary, a sort of buffer genre more or less halfway to fiction. When newsreel and Feature merge . . . I'm blunting my mind trying to cypher this through and ending up in anticlimax every time. I guess you do have to be there. I feel on firmer ground saying that the text is using filmic analogies for what has been happening all through *Beautiful Losers*, a veritable bible of miasmal mixture or generic instability. Just look at part of the exit from Book Two, which has escaped F.'s narrative control:

(DOLLY IN TO CLOSE-UP OF THE RADIO ASSUMING THE FORM OF PRINT)
—This is the radio speaking. Good evening. The radio easily interrupts this book to bring you a recorded historical news flash: TERRORIST LEADER AT LARGE.

(CLOSE-UP OF RADIO EXHIBITING A MOTION PICTURE OF ITSELF)
—This is the radio speaking. Eeek! Tee hee! This is the ah ha ha, this is the hee hee, this is the radio speaking. Ha ha ha ha ha, oh ho ho ho, ha ha ha ha ha ha, it tickles, it tickles! (SOUND EFFECT; ECHO CHAMBER) This is the radio speaking. Drop your weapons! This is the Revenge of the Radio (240-41).

Typing out this passage (simpler to chuckle over than to analyse in terms of, say, the various genres playing in it) is a good reminder that *Beautiful Losers* never takes itself seriously, never plays the same game, for long. Which is not to say that it should not be taken seriously. The novel is light-hearted as Eastern sages whose jokes may be doors to wisdom. The narrator of Book One would love to be able to "stand on some holy mountain of experience" and "sweetly nod [his] Chinese head over" the betrayals and outrages of his life (7). In the journey paradigm, he has achieved that stance as Book One winds down, but what I like best about the sentence-long section 51 is not the way it fits the journey-to-enlightenment pattern by detailing the narrator's empty-headed openness, his acceptances ("artificial limb accepted,

Hong Kong sex auxiliaries accepted, money confessions accepted, wigs of Celanese acetate accepted"); what I really like is that somebody, whether author or narrator or both, cannot resist inserting a brief satiric variation into this litany: "Zen Ph.D. tolerated" (145). Thus the hypnotised might signal the hypnotist that s/he has not completely relinquished control. Thus the colonized might warn the imperialist of a stormy rule to come.

The style of Book Three, "Beautiful Losers, an Epilogue in the Third Person" is not neutral. It borrows from both previous narrators, but is governed by neither of them. So the narrative surface of most of Book Three is smooth and calm. F. and his friend are and are not what they were. The borders between their identities have corroded and they have merged. Edith had been revealed as a contemporary incarnation of Isis in Book Two, and now she is and is not the woman in the fast car, naked below the waist, who picks up the hitch-hiker who used to be her husband. The moccasins she wears show that the identity of Catherine has been folded in. Understanding *how* the newsreel walks "right into plot" may not be necessary; the corrosive results, in these destabilized identities, are clear enough. Now the Feature is not going to stay put.

In downtown Montreal, next to the System Theatre at the Main Shooting and Game Alley, the climax of the book plays to an audience of generic people drawn by the sense that "Action was suddenly (not in the theatres but) in the streets" (256). They are treated to an unusual experience as the composite old man begins to dissolve "from the inside out" (259), and to reassemble himself,

> And at that point where he was most absent, that's when the gasps started, because the future streams through that point, going both ways. That is the beautiful waist of the hourglass! That is the point of Clear Light! Let it change forever what we do not know" (258)!

The finale of this virtuoso display is his reassembling of himself "into—into a movie of Ray Charles."

Then he enlarged the screen, degree by degree, like a documentary on the Industry. The moon occupied one lens of his sunglasses, and he laid out his piano keys across a shelf of the sky, and he leaned over them as though they were truly the row of giant fishes to feed a hungry multitude. A fleet of jet planes dragged his voice over us who were holding hands.
—Just sit back and enjoy it, I guess.
—Thank God it's only a movie.
—Hey! cried a New Jew, laboring on the lever of the broken Strength Test. Hey. Somebody's making it (258-259)!

Only a movie, eh? A movie must have got crossed with the northern lights. But there would have been food lineups after that original miracle of loaves and fishes too, and people urging others to "Eat up" and only much later wondering then finally realizing Who was catering, and How. Linda Hutcheon complains that this Montreal audience isn't taking the message (32), but I say give them time.

Meanwhile, this crowd of strangers, this melded cross-section of contemporary urbanites, is holding hands and enjoying themselves, and there is no missing the happy ending even if it *is* understated in contemporary slang. In *Savage Fields* Dennis Lee has no use for this ending, none for the whole Epilogue. In fact he feels the essential action of the book is over before the resumption of Catherine's story in Book Two. The rest is copout. But Lee's *Savage Fields* translates *Beautiful Losers* into terms that fit an argument: contemporary "world" and "earth" (roughly, technology and nature) are locked in vicious competition. The no-outlet argument itself is sobering in its plausibility, and there is much in *Beautiful Losers* that supports it, but the novel flies free of it, right to the end. I'm tempted to adapt (freely) the term polyphony (in "Polyphony: Enacting a Meditation," Lee's essay on poetics) to describe its flight: polyphony orchestrated as by the Queen of Hearts in Wonderland.

The happy ending is not the ending. Two brief unconnected passages remain, and they bounce out of the third person. One of them, "rented to the Jesuits" (259) puts forth a case for

59

Catherine's canonization, and the other seems to me to wind back to the opening when everything was up in the air. The last sentence, as George Bowering points out in "A Great Northward Darkness: The Attack on History in Recent Canadian Fiction," is a couplet (7). It's also a very belated welcome to the reader, a welcome to melancholy and longing. It's an ending, calm but not restful, that wants to be played with. Or perhaps the whole novel needs to be played again with this ending in mind.

*

The whole of *Beautiful Losers* seems to stream through certain set-piece passages composed of the contradictory "stresses of existence" that characters and readers alike must wrestle with. These passages are part of a self-reflexive inquiry into order and chaos in life and art. They interest a reader in something other than how the plot turns out. They magnetize a reader's attention with the prospect of meaning, even a "necklace of incomparable beauty and unmeaning" (18); with an offer of "the exercise of a kind of balance in the chaos of existence" (101); with "a dance of masks" in which "there was but one mask but one true face which was the same and which was a thing without a name which changed and changed into itself over and over" (140); with the lure of "the sound of the sounds (heard) together" (160).

The well-known passages so abbreviated, those wellsprings of aesthetic sense, supplement and connect with each other, and they might all be felt to meet in the statement of faith that F. calls "the sweet burden of my argument" (167). This is the poem, "God is alive. Magic is afoot," that has been wonderfully served in a musical setting by Buffy St. Marie. Actually F.'s message involves a further leap, beyond faith in human creative capacity to the divine source of it all. But in this constellation of remarkable passages lies the meaning of *Beautiful Losers* for those who feel that the novel has something important to say, something the mind can hold and carry away. Both the narrator and F. (the latter in a weak moment), feel the pull of this sort of kernelized meaning. The appetite survives in the "part of (the narrator's) mind which buys solutions" (135), in the "American" part of F.'s mind that wants "to tie my life up with a visit" (45). Small wonder a reader should feel his/her desire for order exercised by this book.

The saint-artist's "exercise of a kind of balance in the chaos of existence," that visionary "necklace of incomparable beauty and unmeaning" and the rest—these are not images of easy harmony, or they wouldn't be as seductive as they are. But all the same they are reassuring figures which link or contain the members of chaos, lending them at least the illusion of coherence. If God is alive the whole shebang makes sense because the lamented "transcendental signified" never really died. So it's plausible to read *Beautiful Losers* as a modernist novel with an underlying drive towards organic unity because the novel powerfully sponsors that sort of response. The "celestial manifestation" (75) of the "Epilogue" would then be the plot's fulfillment of the principle of harmony under whose influence one threads the parts of the novel as beads on a necklace. But if the novel were meant to inhere in those transcendent passages, I don't believe that, line by line, page by page, the experience of reading it would involve such continual readjustment and surprise and joyous evasion of a critic. *Beautiful Losers* will slake the thirst for meaning, for resolution, but only in a reader partially amnesiac.

A few passages that connect, however compelling, are not the book. Leonard Cohen has delegated no one to speak for him; neither do the collected voices of the novel add up to Writ. Sometimes the narrative mask all but dissolves to let us see through the words to the man who wrote them, as when a voice one almost seems to recognize cries,

> O reader, do you know that a man is writing this? A man like you who longed for a hero's heart. In arctic isolation a man is writing this, a man who hates his memory and remembers everything, who was once as proud as you . . . ." (108).

The suddenness of this, rather than any inconsistency with what else the volatile narrator has been saying, persuades me that the author is flirting with self-revelation (if such can be said of one

61

who all but slides into the bones of Eliot's drowned sailor, Phlebas the Phoenician, "once handsome and tall as you" 85). It makes more poignant the appeal to a common experience of exile from bravery and purity of intention. A man like me, only too conscious of his limitations, made *Beautiful Losers* out of his longing. Writer and reader, narrators and characters—we're all in this wilderness together, and only the characters emerge.

Writer and reader are again together, abandoned, in the last passage of the novel, where the melancholy tone is heard again. Those reassuring passages with the family face are not the whole picture; F. speaks only for himself; there is no resting in, say, "God is alive. Magic is afoot;" meaning is not only fluid but collaborative, not only collaborative but reconstituted with each reading. The desire for order is so palpable in the minds of both narrator/characters, those chips off the old block, that any conclusions they reach ought to be suspect. Their cries of metaphysical loneliness and prayers to silent gods ring through *Beautiful Losers*. Here is the narrator of Book One straining against mental and physical constipation to thread (or comma splice) some faulty logic into a charm against loneliness: "Please make me empty, if I'm empty then I can receive, if I can receive it means it comes from somewhere outside of me, if it comes from outside of me I'm not alone! I cannot bear this loneliness. Above all it is loneliness" (41). F.'s generalization of the theme appears in a prayer abruptly inserted into the letter to his friend:

> (O Father, Nameless and Free of Description, lead me from the Desert of the Possible. . . . Dear Father accept this confession: we did not train ourselves to Receive because we believed there wasn't Anything to Receive and we could not endure with this Belief) (190).

The joy of "God is alive. Magic is afoot" is not punctured but it pales beside the pain of a mind bereft of certainties in Book One, and it's undercut in Book Two when F. all but admits that spiritual loneliness scares human beings into affirmation. In the words of Don McKay, written in the margin of a draft of this essay, "the 'God is alive' passage is one spiritual posture among many, orally and aurally compelling but of no greater weight than the others in a democracy of spiritualities."

Beautiful Losers has a great deal to do with the response of artists like F. to the lonely wrack of contemporary life. The novel is largely about the principles and workings of the weird "system" that F. is using to mould out of the lumpen clay of his friends superbeings with perfect bodies and wide open minds. He wants things different, "any old different" (199), and not just for the hell of it. "What is most original in a man's nature," runs one of his aphorisms, "is often that which is most desperate. Thus new systems are forced on the world by men who simply cannot bear the pain of living with what is" (59). A poet's allegiance, the passage goes on, "Is to the notion that he is not bound to the world as given, that he can escape the painful arrangement of things as they are" (59). F.'s examples are two "creators" not often associated: Hitler and Jesus.

Hitler? This might sound a little like John Cage saying that the music of Beethoven is every bit as acceptable to him as a cowbell, except that Cage is not putting the holocaust into play, not introducing the "unspeakable" subject (Yanofsky 31). If you rethink music along with Cage, any noise is worth listening to, but is there a rethinking capable of erasing the difference between Jesus and Hitler? The plot shows that F. is not talking through his hat, at least. He and Edith would likely be as happy to go three in a tub with Jesus as with Hitler, though Jesus might not bring the soap. Hitler's soap is human soap; it's six million Jews. In what sort of system is this a comic turn? In the system called *Beautiful Losers*. F. is not laughing. His "lust for secular gray magic" (175) makes him covet that soap. He feeds on *any* power.

To write his letter, F. says, he has "had to stretch my mind back into areas bordered with barbed wire, from which I spent a lifetime removing myself" (164). He never suffered any scruples to interfere with the gratification of his lust for life, and the Argentinian hotel scene shows that he has erased the border between good and evil. Theoretically, he should be far from

Jesuit territory, then, away from the Christian system with its tales of Hero and Adversary in settings of heaven and hell, but he isn't.

The Jesuits use ghastly paintings of hell (in the seventeenth-century narrative of Book One) to frighten the Indians out of their own less dualistic system into "a new kind of loneliness" (87), the death of their heaven. The novel makes this tragedy moving, as I've said, but it does not stay on the side of the losers. Renting the end of the book to the Jesuits is not the first sign that what they stand for, unfair players and winners though they are, may have its admirable side. The narrator of Book One includes in his paean of homage to the Jesuits ("because they saw miracles") a section it's easy to skip or forget, unless one comes to it thinking of F. and Hitler:

> Homage to the vaulted halls where we knelt face to face with the shit-enhaloed Accuser of the World. . . . Homage to those old torturers who did not doubt the souls of their victims, and, like the Indians, allowed the power of the Enemy to nourish the strength of the community (106).

Like F., though hardly in the same way, the Jesuits have congress with the devil. In a novel of collapsing identities it shouldn't be surprising that Hitler's exit leaves behind "the vague stink of [the Adversary's] sulphurous flatulence" (195). There is no passage celebrating the fact that the Devil is afoot, but the narrators of Books One and Two both fold into their thinking his energy of darkness.

If God is alive, is F. even on his side? In the orgy that climaxes with the Danish Vibrator, F.'s "Pygmalion tampering" (195) with Edith is revealed. "You've gone against God" (176), she says to him, placing him in the Archetypal Rebel camp, and that association is extended in a passage that darkly parodies his friend's vision of unity, early in the novel, created by the "needle" of his mind that when relaxed sews everything together: "everything which has existed and does exist, we are part of a necklace of incomparable beauty and unmeaning" (17-18).

This "comforting message, a beautiful knowledge of unity," has to be matched with the perspective of F.'s contrasting needlework in Book Two. Then one understands why F. might consider it "some glimmering of a fake universal comprehension" (17). Maybe he hates to see a student backslide; maybe he's jealous. His ambition may be well-meaning but it's also, as overreaching always is, disastrous:

> Call me Dr. Frankenstein with a deadline. I seemed to wake up in the middle of a car accident, limbs strewn everywhere, detached voices screaming for comfort, severed fingers pointing homeward, all the debris withering like sliced cheese out of Cellophane—and all I had in the wrecked world was a needle and thread, so I got down on my knees, I pulled pieces out of the mess and I started to stitch them together. I had an idea of what a man should look like, but it kept changing. I couldn't devote a lifetime to discovering the ideal physique. All I heard was pain, all I saw was mutilation. My needle going so madly, sometimes I found I'd run the thread right through my own flesh and I was joined to one of my own grotesque creations—I'd rip us apart—and then I heard my own voice howling with the others, and I knew that I was also truly part of the disaster. But I also realized that I was not the only one on my knees sewing frantically. There were others like me, making the same monstrous mistakes, driven by the same impure urgency, stitching themselves into the ruined heap, painfully extracting themselves—(186-87)

Is he thinking of his failure when he shouts "connect nothing" in response to his friend's necklace vision of unity. "Place things side by side on your arborite table, if you must, but connect nothing" (18)! If F. were a contemporary writer/theorist like, say, Robert Kroetsch, he might shout "Metonymy, not metaphor!" You could see him touting the "postmodernist" fragmentary text over the "modernist" integral one, a stance more consistent with the message that borders between genres may be corroded than with the message that God is alive and the first term of meaning is still in place. But the point is that, given his confession, given his overreaching, who's going to put much faith in F. as a creator, as a saint? His system is a botch.

Or is it? Now we're only listening to the dark side. This reading has in fact risked abandoning balance in order to explore it. There comes a time to put aside the search for consistency in F.'s system and resolution in this novel, to put aside all that irritable reaching after fact & reason. "Shhh" is

> the sound made around the index finger raised to the lips. Shhh, and the roofs are raised against the storm. Shhh, the forests are cleared so the wind will not rattle the trees. Shhh, the hydrogen rockets go off to silence dissent and variety" (157).

Shhh, the trickster text will now behave itself. Resisting that step aside into irony doesn't necessarily mean deciding whose side F. is on. It means keeping the option open.

"We rejoiced to learn that mystery was our home" (164), F. recalls to his friend (and the pronoun welcomes the reader). Their home is this novel. With a true mystery there is nothing to do but play. Mystery is life in the best novels, those tests of the centre's cohesion, and play is the creative process at its most cooperative and least judgmental. Of course, by accommodating Hitler, Cohen becomes one of those heroes of the edge, in the words of Michael Ondaatje's "White Dwarfs," "who shave their moral so raw/ they can tear themselves through the eye of a needle" (*Rat Jelly* 70). He pushes his system right up to the edge of the tolerable. He goes where I can follow him only in fiction, and even then not without a shudder.

What is it like to get near the Source, to move into "death," and return to tell about it? "I," in Ed Dorn's *Slinger,* sometime secretary to Parmenides, begins his account this way:

> First off,
> the lights go out on Thought
> and an increase in the thought of thought,
> plausibly flooded w/ darkness,
> in the shape of an ability to hear Evil praised . . . (Book IIII)

Is it something akin to this detachment, this revision of priorities—radical as that of Lazarus, returned from the grave in Browning's "An Epistle of Karshish" and now indifferent to the deaths of children—that permits a reader to accept Hitler and his soap as integral to *Beautiful Losers,* as merely the most extreme of Cohen's many courageous outrages of convention and taste? Or is it slackness, failure of the imagination to grasp the enormity of Cohen's glibness about the holocaust? The former, I think, after soul-searching, but my confidence on the subject is given to slippage.

*

I find myself thinking how reluctant I have become to stand away and generalize about *Beautiful Losers.* But then I have always felt a perverse identification with an improbable character imagined by Jorge Luis Borges. Funes the Memorious suffered a knock on the head that left him with phenomenal capacities of perception and memory but with absolutely no generalizing capacity.

> With no effort, he had learned English, French, Portuguese and Latin. I suspect, however, that he was not very capable of thought. To think is to forget differences, generalize, make abstractions. In the teeming world of Funes, there were only details, almost immediate in their presence (*Labyrinths* 66).

In another sort of story, like *Middlemarch,* this is the mind of a human computer, the arid systematiser of the Key To All Mythologies. But Borges makes the mind and thus the world of Funes sensuously rich. Funes is totally attuned to the solid bloody landscape. It is almost as though when everything rearranged itself in his brain he found himself somehow again unfallen. I think it is true and maybe even valuable to say of *Beautiful Losers* that its life-blood is the love and pain that saturate it. If the final note of the novel were the only one that lasted, then pain would be uppermost, but I haven't been arguing the importance of that ending to assert its primacy or finality. The novel thwarts a teleological reading, after all. I need the mind of Funes to detect how this novel means, as any novel means that teems enough to qualify as a world. From generalizing I lately feel the pull to plunge back in, especially into the riddling parts, like this bit of F.'s arousal script, with his commentary:

> "SEND ME ANOTHER Rupture-Easer so I will have one to change off with. It is enabling me to work top speed at the press machine 8 hrs a day," this I threw in for sadness, for melancholy soft flat groin pad which might lurk in Edith's memory swamp as soiled lever, as stretched switch to bumpy apotheosis wet rocket come out of the fine print slum where the only trumpet solo is grandfather's stringy cough and underwear money problems (182).

This is writing of precision in the nonsense tradition of carnivalizing sense, very much alive in the work of contemporary inheritors like the so-called "language" writers. It isn't hard to contextualize these lines so, nor to connect words like "apotheosis" and "rocket" with the journey of the soul (in the "birchbark rocket") on which the narrator hopes he will be joining Catherine. But the mystery is local in passages like this. I know I could do something approximate, quite a lot actually, in the way of accounting for the madcap melancholy this one creates, but ultimately these crafted non sequiturs elude any zoo of language and I throw in the towel. I shut up, not in defeat but respect.

*

Quel age as-tu?
Quel age as-tu?
Quel age,
Quel age,
Quel age as-tu?

For Leonard Cohen on the occasion of his 60th birthday

Works Cited

Barreto-Rivera, Rafael. *Nimrod's Tongue*. Toronto: Coach House Press, 1985.

Borges, Jorge Luis, *Labyrinths: Selected Stories and Other Writings*. New York: New Directions, 1964.

Bowering, George, "A Great Northern Darkness: The Attack on History in Recent Canadian Fiction." *Imaginary Hand: Essays*. Edmonton: NeWest, 1988.

Cage, John. *Silence*. Middletown, Conn.: Wesleyan University Press, 1939.

Cohen, Leonard. *Beautiful Losers*. Toronto: McClelland and Stewart, 1966.

Dorn, Edward. *Slinger*. Berkeley: Wingbow, 1968.

Eliot, T.S. *Collected Poems 1909-1935*. New York: Harcourt, Brace, 1936.

Griffin, Susan M. and William Veeder, eds. *The Art of Criticism: Henry James on the Theory and the Practice of Fiction*. Chicago and London: University of Chicago Press, 1986.

Hutcheon, Linda. *The Canadian Postmodern*. Toronto: Oxford, 1988.

Lee, Dennis. *Savage Fields: An Essay in Cosmology*. Toronto: Anansi, 1977.

—. "Polyphony: Enacting a Meditation." *Tasks of Passion: Dennis Lee at Mid-Career*. Toronto: Descant, 1982.

Ondaatje, Michael. *Leonard Cohen*. Toronto: McClelland and Stewart, 1970.

—. *Rat Jelly*. Toronto: Coach House, 1973.

—. *Coming Through Slaughter*. Toronto: Anansi, 1976.

Scobie, Steven. *Leonard Cohen*. Vancouver: Douglas & McIntyre, 1978.

—. *Signature Event Cantext*. Edmonton: NeWest, 1989.

Yanofsky, Joel. "Storytelling and the Holocaust." *Brick* 38 (Winter 1990), 30-38.

LOUIS DUDEK

A Note for Leonard Cohen

To borrow vine leaves,
pay for books . . .
(awaken, world of memory)
By a field of timothy,
a stream for perch fishing,
with overhanging boughs . . .
There we sat, the cyclists of those days:
And now you smile, all literature,
our *yong Squyer*,
whose poems are as good as ours
ever were!
Are we to rejoice, in you,
warming our cooled marrow juices
by what you say?
Or, as you imagine, be young with you?
Or call age, a new
kind of power—
an authority over joy?
Nuts, to all that!
You may be free, of us, be perfect
pitiful, without a thought, as we
will look here and there
for such crumbs as still
half satisfy: but you are
ourselves, and suffer the same brief
no, no more—the whole story
takes in the lot of us.

DOUGLAS FETHERLING

Art Criticism

Je suis ici pour faire des achats de dynamite.—Blaise Cendrars

There are no guarantees
that anything will last
especially when you use
these inferior materials

Thick chemical gesso
slides onto recycled canvas
one coat horizontal
the next vertical;
as soon as one dries,
another arrives to
contradict it.

I can't stand the silence.
My ears chafe waiting
for the tune of a catchy explosion.
I am the neighbourhood dynamiter
who never knows when opportunity
might strike. One must always
be alert and heavily armed
against success and its enemies.

This is how I am.
I have no patience
with craft for its own sake
not like the old
Chinese man standing
in his garden every morning
applying more red lacquer
to his coffin.

When the surface is hard
and shiny like a beetle
he will be venerated as only
the ancient dead can be.

I will be scattered over a wide area.
Parts of me may never be found.

Composing in the mid-eighties
Photo by Dominique Issermann

RAYMOND FILIP

The Only Montreal Poet
Who Doesn't Know Leonard Cohen

Never close enough to call him "Leonard," he has never taken me down to his place by The Main to touch my imperfect body with his mind. Thank Yahweh. The armor of fame protects an image. If you attack Leonard Cohen, then you are jealous. If you fill his ears with praise, then you are a servile flatterer. How to avoid such dialectical pitfalls in spelling out why you are, and are not a fan? I am guided by the beautiful banality of one private encounter with Cohen in the flesh.

It was a hot summer evening in 1985. I parked my Honda 650 motorcycle in front of his open door on Marie-Anne St. The house lights were on. There he stood, rewinding audio equipment on his kitchen table. He greeted me with far-away eyes. I introduced myself. Recognition clicked, slowly, in his long-term memory. Then, to my great relief, Leonard Cohen permitted this ectomorphic biker dressed in a leather jacket, shorts, and running shoes to enter his interior. Specifically: his washroom.

First, this story requires rewinding in order to explain where I was coming from. I had initially met Leonard Cohen in the sixties within the pages of a "dirty" book. *Beautiful Losers* with its erotic cover and irreverent language held secrets which had stimulated the sexual awakening of this Catholic boy reared on Latin, Cardinal Newman, and corporal punishment. An adolescent male must possess the knowledge that carnal drives are not homologous to the animal lust of a bantam cock, but could actually be considered as a sacred fire within the temple of the body. Verdun Catholic High had never taught us that. Nor had I ever fantasized about deflowering Catherine Tekakwitha, a religious symbol, until her transfiguration into a sex symbol by Leonard Cohen. My hormones were hooked. His naughty novel had supposedly been written under the influence of LSD. *Beautiful Losers* definitely deserves the Pharmaprix prize for the best drug-induced writing in Canada.

However, by 1969, with the publication of his selected poems, Cohen was aleady repeating himself with his "lady's man" loop. He had become a false idol, skin deep. A juvenile cleverness disguised metaphysical shallowness. I had grown up and graduated to James Joyce and John Coltrane. Besides, playing the lady's man held disadvantages for a poet with the face of a fighter raised on the streets of Verdun and Point St. Charles, surrounded by tough-looking girls destined for careers as welfare mothers, or waitresses, factory workers, secretaries, nuns, truck drivers' wives, or lady wrestlers. Cohen's "ladies" appeared to be Clairol Girls, art tarts, or monied *baleboostehs*. His words displayed traditional charm and craftsmanship, yet tended to sound similar in the same fashion that Westmount houses maintained their charming exteriors with manicured lawns which all resembled each other after a long walk. Safe homes, safe poems. His world was not my world. I couldn't care less about fucking the maid, or the dark night of the soul on Summit Circle. Cohen expressed middle-class moxie with the ritual prescription of recreational sex and drugs and costume changes. He posed as a typical *artiste* wearing basic black in remembrance of existentialism. His nose droned folkie-dokie ditties about love and social injustices in minor keys to create a "mystical" feel—romantic artifice that serious composers had terminated with the 19th century. *La Vie Boheme a la Cohen.* His various positions suggested nothing azygos. He was better than a sleeping pill. I could not take Leonard Cohen seriously.

Why would a mature man want to masquerade as a Westmount hillbilly? Resisting the forces of Selwyn House and colonial poppycock with vulgate such as "ain't?" Poor darling. True, there ain't no cure for cultural appropriation, and no single socio-economic group enjoys a monopoly on vernacular speech, and writers should be able to cover the whole universe of discourse. It just seemed so unfair and pretentious to affect a working-class accent without any accompanying stigma. Cohen never had to fight for his dignity on the street or in "enlightened" circles. He moved out of upscale Westmount to the downscale East End in

74

order to experience the flip side. If this auto-reverse gesture had flopped, he still would have had the luxury of returning home to the family property. East End natives, to the manure born, spend a lifetime investing in lotto tickets for a chance to taste the good life along Victoria Avenue. Cohen could afford to drop out of Columbia University and go slumming around the globe. If underprivileged children fail to receive an education, they fall down the chute with the industrial waste.

As a student at McGill, I sat at the back of the class, mute, dysphoric, outwardly asking no questions, taking notes, handing in assignments on time, communicating via paper for four years, too afraid to reveal my idiolect. Whenever I opened my mouth, bluntness was mistaken for rudeness. Charming exteriors had never been a part of my environment. Leonard Cohen was omnipresent in term papers, libraries, bookstores, record shops, knapsacks . . . the personal savior of spoiled brats. The hippies on campus were hypocrites with the accent on "hip", accustomed to having things their own way, future power brokers. The pretty boys and girls intellectualized so glibly about war and hunger and inequality: none of which they had ever suffered. They dressed down in tie-dyed blue jeans, smoked pot, and pilgrimaged back to Mother Earth on weekends or holidays at their parents' cottage. I saw the yuppy in them.

I dressed up in corduroy, proud to be accepted by McGill. The idyllic campus with its exotic trees and contemplative grass and Three Graces Fountain and peripatetic squirrels and Mount Royal in the background beckoning poets to hunt for missing muses all presented a respectable change from gray Verdun. Spit-covered sidewalks and schoolyards and unpredictable fires had shaped my voice. The Atwater and Wellington tunnels which lead in and out of Verdun and Point St. Charles may as well serve as the walls of an open prison. These two tunnels enclose "bad" neighborhoods with low rent and low life, arsonists, bums, rats, row housing like jail cells, boarded-up windows in condemned buildings, factories, warehouses, stores, garbage in back lanes smelling of cat piss, dog shit on streets, torn newspapers, crushed beer cans, cigarette butts, broken glass, broken homes, broken lives.

I pedaled back and forth from Verdun to McGill on a 3-speed CCM bicycle, uphill and downhill, in and out of the Atwater or Wellington tunnels, clear through until winter, wondering if the day would ever arrive when I could say goodbye to all that? I worked so hard. I would retreat to the washroom of the McLennan Library and break down into tears out of extreme loneliness and exhaustion. McGill was so Anglo, so mercantile, so status quo. The hallowed halls bred a shadiness and superiority complex as fraudulent as the land grant of ye ol' beaver bugger: James McGill. *Grandescunt Aucta Labore*, my ass. The snobs would have died in working class boots.

It took this alumni member 16 more years to escape from Verdun, a checkered path of poetry books and university degrees. The graduation line and the unemployment line kept merging. My guitar remained the sole guaranteed money-maker, more so than any diploma. I ended up giving private lessons to the pampered pickers in the West Island, or Hampstead, or Westmount. Yes, the superbrats requested Leonard Cohen tunes. Easy to play: "A minor" poet. I had to watch my "ain'ts" and "Fuck, man's," and retain a civil tone while sinking into the plush carpeting of dens surrounded by polished silver, china, antique furniture, expensive paintings and stereo systems, haggling with mummy or daddy over why there was no cash around the house again this week to pay for junior's music lessons. Using this method, I earned a living off rich dodos insufficiently endowed to teach themselves cheap music.

This is what Leonard Cohen represents to me: double leverage. Only he could pull off a coup such as speaking his songs and winning the Juno Award as the best male vocalist of 1993. "It's only in a country like this . . . "

High or low standards are peripheral in the art of writing songs for teenagers of all ages. That is the "message." The rest is backstage politics, PR games, the public image so much more important than the perfect metaphor. Try Purolator Express for urgent pronouncements. Or send every wealthy poet preaching

76

love and zen for direction through darkness to the most treacherous corner of the Wellington tunnel and make him or her recite proletarian verse from 9-to-5, (plus overtime), as punishment for being born well-connected! At least Cohen possessed the *chutzpah* to turn his back on the family business and gamble with the flash-and-trash pop industry. The high priest of Montreal minstrelsy saw the light: Laser Karaoke with on-screen lyrics!

Leonard Cohen was in the right place at the right time, pushing the right buttons, just as adult culture and the pleasure craft of literature was beginning to sink. He crossed over on the electronic flood of youth culture and rock-'n-roll thought control. The charge continues through the plugs, amps, cables, channels, serial ports, patchbays, ethernets, multitrackers, and satellite dishes for SMPTE visionaries, MIDI maestros, and CD-ROM rhymers in the mosh pit of mass culture.

Where else could our paths have crossed except at McGill? The occasion was Louis Dudek's retirement party. Dudek had opened the starting gate for Cohen in 1956 by publishing his debut collection of poems: *Let Us Compare Mythologies*. Dudek originated from the East End of Montreal. He had elevated himself to the rank of full professor. His roots still showed in his accidentally dropped "g's", or in his prefacing of scholarly statements with "Hey, man." His concerns ranged from hidden mysteries such as Atlantis to the withdrawn student in his office hiding a history of abuse. We both shared a love of learning. I would sit for hours fascinated by his tales about famous Canadian poets—including "Leonard." Cohen had frequently visited him in Verdun where Dudek had lived for 17 years in the gentrified west end. I attempted to picture Cohen and Dudek strolling together along the aqueduct where I had played as a child. I don't remember seeing them. Apparently, they had compared notes over a manuscript which would eventually grace book shelves as *Spice Box of Earth*.

It is hard to embrace the notion that Leonard Cohen, the voluptuary, was ever a "disciple" of Louis Dudek: the trafficker in ideas. Cohen has dedicated several poems to Irving Layton, but none to Dudek. "Mentor" is another term often adopted by the press to describe the relationship between Dudek and his former students who happen to write books. The whiter the hair, the more likely is the promotion from professor to Mentor Emeritus. Dudek himself spurns such hagiography. He does not believe in veneration or awards. They cause friction and fraction.

Also, not every student is a lost Telemachus. My work had already appeared within the prestigious print of the *Queen's Quarterly* before I had even enrolled in Dudek's CanLit course. Furthermore, we constantly exchanged friendly fire over poetics. He advocated the long poem as a pantheon for continuous grandiloquence. I argued that our age of Sound and Vision no longer demands epic literature. Musically-trained poets are taking over from paper-trained poets. Lyric verse has always uplifted the human heart and mind through a sweeping arpeggio of thoughts and emotions over time. The psalms of the Bible helped to establish a code of worship; the lyres of Sappho and Pindar spun Greece into gold; the Provencal troubadours sang Europe out of the Dark Ages; the Elizabethan Songbook refined England through the words of William Shakespeare and Anonymous; Walt Whitman sang himself and America into being—as did his Afro-American counterpart Langston Hughes, who bestowed dignity upon black diction with his blame-it-on-the-blues eloquence. Even Allen Ginsberg has settled into senior citizenship with chants and chimes. And what of the voice that is great within Canada? Leonard Cohen?

I am sure Louis Dudek also subjected Cohen to this initiation rite of contrary motion. A loved and respected teacher, Dudek could ignite debates about aesthetics with the pinpoint accuracy of a pivotal flame thrower. Thanks to his introduction service, I was to meet his most famous pupil.

The retirement party took place at the Faculty Club. The room bubbled with wine and cheese and cerebral chuckles. Ken Norris read an encomium. Then Dudek addressed an intimate gathering of friends and associates. In his chipper manner, he cracked jokes about retirement and quoted funny epitaphs (which I cannot remember). He pointed out how much he had appreciated the "individuality" of his colleagues over the years. Then it was over. Short and sweet. Nobody took attendance, but the head count gradually diminished with the contents of the punch bowl. Sip, gossip. Sip, gossip. Hold onto your sandwich wedge and pick your way through an unconscionable array of crusty pedants, imaginary slights, pomposity, and silent cuts in the anechoic world of academics.

Enter: Leonard Cohen.

He walked in just in time. Bill Furey, his guardian angel, escorted him. Dudek looked astonished and delighted. Both were beamingly happy to see each other again. They chatted for about five minutes. The corner of every eye from every angle of the room stole a peek at the latecomer. Buzz, buzz. "Is that Leonard Cohen?" Or "Oh look, Leonard is here."

I had witnessed Leonard Cohen afoot in Montreal twice before. In the late '70s, he had made a cameo appearance in the audience for an Al Purdy poetry reading at Vehicule Art Gallery. The second sighting had occurred at a local bookstore during a signing session for *Book of Mercy*.

My observer status ended when Cohen elected to schmooze with Ken Norris, Bill Furey, and myself in a fraternal huddle. The conversation centered around his music. He talked freely about recording. No patronizing tone: a sign of greatness. His equanimity surprised me. He treated us as peers, the boys, poets on the same footing. My class bias began to dissolve with his warmth. I was not tempted to dispute the political correctness of populism. Good vibes ruled the moment. Leonard Cohen was successful in his obstacle course; I was successful in mine.

Then the graying lady's man with the dashing good looks had to rush off again. He offered to drive us home.

"Where do you live, Ray?"

"Verdun."

"Bye, Ray," Bill Furey intervened.

"It's okay. I like to walk," I replied.

"Drop in any time," Cohen added in parting.

"Oh . . . ," I made a mental note of his exit line. "Okay. I will."

And I did.

That brings us back to his doorstep. I was still not sure whether to address him as "Leonard," or "Mr. Cohen," or whether he would even remember me from Dudek's retirement party a few months back. He was in the middle of taping something on a portable recorder. Hence, the far-away eyes. I was interrupting the creative process. But my bladder felt like a hydro dam about to burst after ingesting several litres of club soda all day.

"I'll only be a second," I promised.

"Okay," Cohen agreed in a state of distraction.

"Thanks."

A quick on-the-way-to-the-washroom glance revealed an austere setting: no polishing silver, no antique furniture, no thick carpeting, no expensive paintings, nothing eyecatching beyond the electronic hardware spread across his bare table. Cohen's living space radiated the atmosphere of a monastery converted into a Radio Shack.

On the immediate right, his washroom awaited customers. I noticed that the tub was filled with blue water. I dared not stick my finger inside Leonard Cohen's blue bathwater. Now I really felt like an intruder. Did he think I was one of those kooks who rummage through celebrity garbage cans? Or an autograph hound? Or a hustler armed with demos? I tried not to urinate too loudly since his tape recorder lay only a few feet away. Turned on? Was Cohen sampling ambient sounds? Or composing with chance operations? The only sound I heard was the song of my copious piss, embarrassingly long and raucous. I aimed around the edges of the toilet bowl in order to reduce the hiss. Then the phenomenology of it all hit me. Here I am in Leonard Cohen's toilet. I don't know him, he doesn't know me. I could be another Mark Chapman out to murder him. Or he could be another Aleister Crowley about to entice an unsuspecting guest into degenerate acts. Why is Cohen so slippery? To avoid people like me! What *am* I doing here? I confess. I have lied. Leonard Cohen, you don't get my entertainment dollar anymore. You are a poet for beginners: student studs. I will go home and listen to Glenn Gould, Arvo Pärt, or Arnold Schönberg: artists of genuine profundity and complexity in their spiritual quests. The only monk I adore is Thelonius Monk. You bathe in publicity while non-commercial "stars" go unrecognized by the musically illiterate masses who live in Lalaland. Fair play? Could *you* perform "The Goldberg Variations?" Or "Giant Steps?" "Suzanne," your song of songs, is an elementary lullaby that eases basketcases through the night. You and Dr. Ruth and 1-976-LUST. Sexual awakening lasts a lifetime for some basketcases. Keep that phallocentric faith. Have you ever flirted with the idea of writing in more difficult genres? A rock opera? A musical? Stretching the parameters of song within a concept album? Or learning jazz? You're not my man with a cop-out such as "Jazz Police." Have you ever heard Oscar Peterson's very lyrical *Canadiana Suite?* Do your ears get lost within the cleavage of a bitonal chord such as F 13#11? Are you a "pop artist" because of your limitations? If not, then why prostitute your talent to please the crowd? If the crowd can't sing-a-long, they won't buy it. If the crowd has to look up words, they won't buy it. That is pretty limiting. The Starmaker Machine produces "tar" with the regularity of an automatic teller. The machine does not inherently run on brilliance. As Ray Charles once said on the Arsenio Hall Show: "You don't have to be good to be famous." (Charles humbly admitted that he was not as "good" as the piano virtuoso Art Tatum known to jazz aficionados but not to Pepsi drinkers.) The greatness of a star depends upon the distance of the observer. It is all relative. HURRY UP PLEASE IT'S TIME. Poets. Maybe I should have stopped for a nature call at McDonald's instead. Anyway. I got it out of me. There.

I zippered up.

"Hope I didn't disturb you?" I stepped into his kitchen.

"It's alright."

Cohen had remained stationed at his table. His audio gear fully preoccupied his attention. He was obviously slaved to tape, laboring over new material, under pressure to produce, waiting for me to leave so he could play back his song-in-progress. The melody had probably been snatched out of a breeze while humming *Om mani padme hum* and beholding a jewel inside a lotus. He had been a vessel for the second verse which passed through

81

him on a yacht while cruising in the Zone of the Unmanifest near The Bermuda Triangle. The third verse had to be sweated out inside a woodshed in Warsaw. A bonus fourth verse had struck him out of nowhere over the waters of the Atlantic on an overnight flight from Greece to New York. Further tiny revisions would follow at a Micronesian hotel in Palau. The song would be ready for mass consumption upon discovery of that elusive common chord. Whatever it was, Leonard Cohen knew it. So did any admirer acquainted with the magic of his early texts, or that charming exterior.

"Thanks for everything," I said.

He nodded back, remotely.

So near, yet so far. So much to discuss. I walked outside, put on my helmet, clicked the electric start, and zoomed off as quickly as I had zoomed in. High-speed interfacing. Hey, that's no way to say goodbye! Perhaps if I had been a skinny female on a motorcycle in a leather jacket, shorts, and running shoes. . . .

The courtesy call had been my way of replying to Cohen's invitation. And these words are just my way of wishing a celebrated Montreal poet who I do not know a sincere happy birthday. Beaucoup de candles, rhymes, sparkling wine—and women. You made it to the BIG 60: a sexagenarian with the accent on the sex! Good for the prostate and the heart. Someone who can fill the Montreal Forum with squealy teenies and wrinkled academics on the eve of his 60th birthday must be hip, and not too sclerotic. An author who can perform: two rare gifts.

Leonard Cohen, the two hands of God congratulate you.

JUDITH FITZGERALD

very much like singing

When it all comes crumbling,
it comes in the name of down-and-dirty
deliverance and you know it.

Sweet whiff of memory percolates
through strata of moonlight: That ol' black
magic don't turn the trick no mo'.

Over at Nighthawk Diner,
he knows I swore
I'd never leave him.

Two hearts forever beating
up on each other, tearing
the lining of every silver promise

wreaking hell-bent havoc
to the tune of the trackmaster;
the upper-handedness raw, edgy, even.

Achtung, body! Now, nova, baby. Black
holes and telephone souls: Put your sweet
lips against the glaze of the good ol' daze.

I came by myself, with neither visual
aids nor aural markers, to identify the corpse:
Guilt insistently functional at four in the morning.

Little labourers in the tower of song,
learning the way brick and mortar mesh
in turning away from the onslaught of self.

This month *Sharks!* hits the museum. Too late,
I think, too late to alleviate approximations of cultural
artifacts, fossils, Western sandwiches on white.

Hold them prayers.
Not one of them cares,
those sharks.

an' sometimes, that ol' ache
cuts deep
    sometimes I cry myself to sleep
    but that don't count for much these days
    life goes by, the jukebox plays

How long does the war go on? We always
knew the one who would lose inhibition
and slit our throats at leisure

in pursuit of excellent pleasure
(or something resembling).
You whom I cannot betray?

I, too, absent all day.
Unfold me, oh, hold me.
I still feel very much like singing.

MICHAEL FOURNIER

Death of a Lemonade Stand

A Sequence for Leonard Cohen

1.

Shade these semblances of memory
in the scarlet hues of the western horizon at dusk;
limit the startling contours in gleaming coal.
Passion is your sum total of relevant verbiage:
you can confirm this with inquiries
of the usual suspects.
Fabricate an 80-proof cosmos thereof:
the boss won't mind, and the taxman
now worships the sun many miles south.

Remember the days when form
was desire's chief modality,
when abstraction was desire at rest,
and rest was pretty regular.

2.

TESTIMONY

Poetry is a loaded gun, and castles
are spilling forth from the heavens
like so much hail, and the buzzards are circling.

In the stillness of the interval
prior to total chaos, the sounds
of distant wind chimes enchant the ear.

It is a hell of a thing, life.

There you are; and then there you are,
functioning somehow.

3.

It is all written in the tea leaves, princess,
we are born, we laugh, we weep
and then the fat lady sings.
There is not much more to it than that:
the situation finds us eminent
in the onslaught of peril.

Ponder the living reach of all these cemetery trees,
consider the distinct character of each.
How easy it sometimes becomes to ascribe to this
glorious world devious paths of revelation.
Yet how much more profoundly brave
to find all the beauty caught up in those branches, and know
they will fall long before the green earth stops still.

Or assess the raw data presented before you
in patterns of all too apparent sequence,
parcel it all discretely and sequester it
into the privacy of your mind,
staring in soundless awe of the likewise
mute, uncomprehending sky.

4.

Being cold, needs it must be bleak, the graveyard
frozen in the clarity of night, each headstone
crowned by an inch or so of fallen snow?
The dead were bold that under them lie flat.
Vague and faraway seems any bleakness, save
in savoring minute details such as places

and dates of births and deaths.
Cold, yes, and the snow
can blind you. You can imagine
never getting out of here alive.

5.

Distance all the passion as
direction is the only reason: I
am not about to argue or descant
anent these salient facts.

Obdurate, I, who possess
this truth, and solid
as the truth is yours.
I am the faith beneath your pedestal.
Do not forget it.

Know me that man who is not ashes, rave
when I shall bear thee to my art's floor!
Stay! even unto distorted parts
that I show thee, irrational.

I shall not be moved.
Time and the elements
are not a problem.

You will recall
the lesson of magic:

something there is
forgets a vast perhaps

perfectly.

6.

Tonight I wrote a marvelous song!
A kind of ecstacy upon which I depend
ditto hangs from the hook of a sickle moon.
Sublime verities gallop through obscure
constellations and Time (a proper noun)
is likewise suspended, and a good thing, too
if any assessment is to be forthcoming.

Yes, goddammit, my song
is one for the ages to ponder,
like runes on an empty hourglass,
like an empty bag of tricks.
My song will be adored in Pittsburgh
where people know what they like,
where circumference of the personal
achieves an acceptable median.

Sometimes unanswered questions ramify
deep into the heart of ineffable truth
and a surer blossom grows
than mere response could ever sow.
I am striving to moderate the vagrancies
of precision.

7.

Last night my mind was on fire
with specific memories. It is
an attribute of grammar that it
permits an expression of plain facts
when the words involved manifest perfect
nonsense in any alternative continuum.
Grammar is of no consequence

to the poet. A bargaining chip,
nothing more. The words,
their rectitude in pattern, are a perfect
sham at best. Books have been written about it.
Things last night were not so restful.
Fire raged where thought sought harbor
and the fleet was in confusion.
I had lost all illusions of tragedy.

GARY GEDDES

Two Poems for Leonard Cohen

DU FU AT CHESTNUT STATION

Waxing cresent moon freighted
with desire; birds taking respite in cedar branches
en route to southern

prefectures. And the poet,
savings exhausted, the gift of shallots
and yams already forgotten,

pauses to write a verse about his ailing horse,
his empty purse, and a gatherer of acorns.
He records what is on his mind

with gaps large enough for a family
to fall through. He came to acquire property,
a rash gesture of welcome over wine,

as if a rugged vista offered better
prospects. Confessing complicity in the unjust
banishment of a friend at court, he blames

his wife and children for the inclement
weather and dire circumstances of this mountain
retreat. His monstrous reflection shatters the waters

of Dragon Pool. He recalls distant brothers,
ponders the final placement of his bones. Sick horse,
hungry eye, extravagant desire.

WHAT DOES A HOUSE WANT?

A house has no unreasonable expectations
of travel or imperialist ambitions;
a house wants to stay
where it is.

A house does not demonstrate
against partition or harbour
grievances;
        a house is a safe
haven, anchorage, place
of rest.

Shut the door on excuses
—greed, political expediency.

A house remembers
its original inhabitants, ventures
comparisons:
        the woman
tossing her hair
on a doorstep, the man
bent over his tools and patch
of garden.

What does a house want?

Laughter, sounds
of love-making, to strengthen
the walls;
        a house
wants people, a permit
to persevere.

A house has no stones
to spare; no house has ever been convicted

of a felony, unless privacy
be considered a crime in the new
dispensation.

What does a house want?

Firm joints, things on the level, water
rising in pipes.

Put out the eyes, forbid
the drama of exits,
entrances; somewhere
in the rubble a mechanism
leaks time,
                         no place
familiar for a fly
to land
on

ALLEN GINSBERG

Leonard Cohen

I went to one of Leonard Cohen's rare New York concerts at Paramount 1993 and was amazed at his gritty realistic voice, relaxed in the abdomen, & the elegant ease of irony with which he thanked overzealous screamers & demanders in the audience—The language bitter, disillusioning like a practiced (Buddhist) Yankee-Canadian, always surprising. He gets better as lyric poet as he gets older, sure sign of youthful mind—the lyrics always evidenced amazing twists & turns of spontaneous inspiration at time of original composition—And the organization it takes to assemble a touring show like that! What a huge work! Wish I could do it but I haven't the skill. I was a little jealous, tho I know it's all a bony burden on Cohen—yet some kind of Bodhisattva Sambhogakaya vow behind his strength in public across the ocean & here.

March 14, 1994 Midnite

CHRISTOF GRAF

Cohen in Nazi-Land

On his recent tour of Germany, Cohen had to perform in the city that he likes least. The city is Berlin. He has invoked Berlin in song on his last two albums. But his '93 concert in the "new old" capitol was less provocative than those in the seventies and eighties. In 1972, the *Berliner Zeitung* was not very pleased with Cohen's fatal statement of Goebbel's "Do you want another war?" But the *Bild Berlin* knew exactly how to report about the concert at the ICC in 1980: "Quiet Leonard is talking loud!" Leonard Cohen asked his fans to separate the ICC and to take home the chairs: "If you see this terrible plastic, you see the dark side of our lives," was his remark about the German Nazi past.

His concert in the Tempodron in Berlin in 1993 was very different. There Leonard Cohen touched the German misery when he sang lyrics like "Give me back the Berlin Wall" while "the audience let the tent in the animal park shake, like drinkers do in their favorite bar at the corner" (*Der Tagesspiegel*). The "magical master of monotony . . . was given a tribute by his audience of all ages with a long lasting applause" (*Berliner Morgenpost*). Cohen's idea of leaving the country quickly almost came to naught because he was so touched by the ovations that were given to him at all six sold-out concerts in Nazi-land.

Cohen knows best what he meant with a lyric like "First we take Manhattan, then we take Berlin." If you are trying to read his mind, you probably interpret what he always wanted to say: "I saw everything, I made up my mind about it, and I am the only one who is responsible for that." Cohen as a prophet? Why not? "'First We Take Manhattan' was about the growth of extremism in everybody's mind. I don't mean in society. I mean in the mind. Everybody has become an extremist. And everybody is ready to defend extreme positions." Cohen is also meeting the spirit of the times of the nineties with his latest album's title song, "The Future," showing the continuation of the just mentioned concept. "Yes," he admitted, "there is a close relationship between "First We Take Manhattan" and "The Future". "The Future" is my struggle with the future. I think it will be more or less like everybody else's struggle with the future. Nobody will experience peace."

Therefore the demand for democracy? "In 'Democracy', which was a song of eighty verses, there was a verse about Europe:

It ain't coming to us European style
Concentration camp behind the smile
It ain't coming from the East
With its temporary feast
As Count Dracula comes strolling down the aisle.

So I was about the only one of my friends who was not rejoicing when the wall came down. I said, this is going to be a mess. Just between us. And I wrote those words around '88-'89. 'Count Dracula comes strolling down the aisle'—that is Europe."

Fritz Haver in his *Me-Sounds* interview, asked Cohen about a song he had been working on that included the line "Give me love or give me Adolf Hitler." Cohen replied: "Well, that song evolved into "The Future." And that is what a lot of people would be saying: give me love or give me Adolf Hitler. They'll be saying it in their hearts. Jews will be saying it. Gentiles will be saying it. The Turks will be saying it. The young Germans will be saying it. They are saying it already, because if there is nothing in the air, if there is no nourishment in the culture as there isn't now, then of course young people will embrace the extremist, this refreshing extremist position, and have the feeling of shaving lotion on their skin. It is enough of the ambiguities, enough of the complexities."

"Nobody will be able to take the freedom. As I say in another song, it looks like freedom but it feels like death, It's something in between I guess. It's Closing Time. It feels like death. It is not death, but it feels like death. And that is gonna scare the shit out of people. It has already. And you can detect it in yourself. This is not a sociological study. This is a reportage of the center of my own life. and I think that is where people are going—into the extreme. It is the only way where there is any comfort. Otherwise, who are we? What are we supposed to be doing? Where is it?"

Even if the media is holding on to the idea that Cohen's *gestalt* is "a bundle of sorrow," they have no choice but to accept that he is a prophet, a prophet of our hearts, despite all the pessimism. "Melancholic melodies, that give a lot of warmth despite their monotony," stated the *Hamburger Abendblatt* after a guest performance in the city-park before 2,000 people. Warmth, far away from pessimism. Even Cohen is not calling himself a pessimist anymore: "Pessimists are those who are always waiting for the rain. As for me, I'm already wet."

Translated by Susanne Lorenz

Frankfurt, Germany, 1988
Photo by Christof Graf

RALPH GUSTAFSON

Three Poems for Leonard

AT THE RUE DE BUCI ONE EVENING

The evening was lovely, the dusk was lovely, the air
Was lovely. Again it was Paris—where they shortchange
Buyers and as bonus are right. But lovely, the crowd,
The people, all of them, thievery elegantly done.
We ran into the noise on the left bank,
On the rue de Buci, music, spontaneous,
Natural, the best of music, loved, the rhythm
Smart as heaven, nine of them, trumpet, cornet,
Trombone, two of each, one for the tuba
Broadside, the clarinet between,
O what a group sophisticated—eight of them
With him out front, bass drum, cymbal, pounded
Like crazy, punctual as fate, the girl with the cornet
Zipping the clarinet's zipper at every break,
Gendarmes shouting to let the automobile through.
It was glory, independence, impregnable joy!

THE TRUE STORY OF THE FLOOD

Ham the son of Noah laughed when born.
The work of the devil. One mourns surely,
Losing heaven, entering this vale of woe
And tears? I yelled so being born,
The wedding of my aunt six houses off
Halted. I knew the world—hung upside down
Slapped in the alien air.

        Ham laughed:
The world washed away! Two and two
The vessel rode the waves, every body
Happy, snugly saved. Lion humped
The lamb, bug the bee. Joy went round,
The circle squared. Doves dropped in. Mrs.
Noah complained. The vessel grounded, hefting
Pitchforks done. Ham begat Chaplin.
All was well.

        Sodom and Gomorrah dried, the lofty
        Karakorams rose, the Dead Sea
        Drained. Dignities of hood
        And gown appeared; solemnities
        Of font and pew. The rainbow shone.
        All was as it had always been,
        Billboards up, markets down,
        Pantries, ethnic enclaves, cleansed.
        Heaven hovered in purest style.

A SPOUT MAKES A JUG

Agreements! lawyers, verbs and inflection,
As if the world was to be yanked into squalling
Assent, in with out, clothes
With emperor. Nature is itself.
He wants her, she, him
As he is, locked in love or not.

It is to be hoped that agreement is fixed
About slaver, big deals, human
Waste? (the sea was excremental
That day you swam to get the shampoo
Out of your hair, you remember? Ischia?
You retched . . .)

On disgusts then, agreement. On how
To break an egg let the world proceed,
Three legs, a stool, four
A chair, what's proposed placed
In context. Down to earth, even
The heavenly host is interesting.

All who agree, raise your hands.

NOEL HARRISON

My Life with Leonard

I'd never heard of him until I listened to a Judy Collins album and "Suzanne" touched my heart. It was 1966. I recorded it and put it out as a single and it got onto the charts. That's how I met Leonard.

It turned out that he and my wife Sara were both born in Montreal on September 19th, 1934. The three of us rode down Sunset Boulevard together in a white convertible Cadillac.

"Noel, take me away from all this," said Leonard.

He moved to Nashville, I to Nova Scotia. Sometime in the seventies I saw a debate advertised at a Canadian college, "Leonard Cohen: Poet or Fraud?" I was quite irritated by the question . . . of course he's a poet, I thought.

I grew older, and more sensible . . . of course he's a fraud, I laughed.

I saw Leonard again a year or two ago, here in Los Angeles. I greeted him warmly. He looked cautiously to the right and to the left. Then at me.

"They'll never catch us," he said.

Happy birthday, Leonard, poet and fraud. You're right. They'll never catch us. Not a chance.

JOY JOHNSTON

Leonard

Leonard is a fine fellow, good companion, and very funny. He came to Nashville in '70, I think. My husband, Bob Johnston, was producing his record and co-managing him with Marty Machat, putting together a band, rehearsing for an international tour. He rented a cabin on 1200 acres in Wadell Hollow, about 30 miles from Nashville. His neighbor/buddy was a moonshiner who had killed a revenuer and done time. Another friend was Kid Marley who managed the cattle and horses on the 1200 acres. He competed in rodeos.

Leonard would give away his money. He paid $75 a month rent, had a single mattress on the floor, a hot plate, picnic table, and a bench. He drove a jeep to ford the creek to get to his place.

He was very interested in others, and different from other artists I had known. Aristocratic, he loved the common folk. We all loved him.

Beautiful women would visit him. He was envied. He was studying Zen and Scientology, always struggling to be free.

I haven't seen him since '86, backstage in San Francisco. I saw him on *Austin City Limits*—I love how he's grown in his music. I always hear rumors about him from other musicians; everyone is interested in what he's doing.

I want to thank him for his work, his kindness to me. I wish him a merry and bright birthday and many more years as the sage he has always been.

TOM KONYVES

For Leonard

How do I love her—
when I got this
you know
mustache headache.

KRIS KRISTOFFERSON

First time I heard Leonard Cohen was in Studio A, Columbia, Nashville, lights out, everybody gone home. Bob Johnston was playing the tape for me. After the first three lines:

"Like a bird on a wire
like a drunk in some midnight choir
I have tried, in my way, to be free . . ."

I said, "That's my epitaph." I was inclined to like him, therefore, before I met him (at some party in somebody's Nashville pad). At one point, after we'd drunk a few, I told him how one of my pilled-up colleagues had figured out that "Bird on a Wire" was the same tune as "Mom & Dad's Waltz" by Lefty Frizell, and how I'd told him that Leonard Cohen probably never even heard of Lefty. Leonard looked at me with a surprised smile. "I love Lefty Frizell!" he exclaimed. "I know all his songs."

So I figured he was worth staying up all night for at the final hours of the Isle of Wight Concert, 1970—the last Woodstock Wannabe, with everyone from Jimi Hendrix to Tiny Tim appearing before a half-million disgruntled spectators sitting in the stink of sweat & urine & garbage from three days of noisy demonstrations by various pissed-off groups of Skinheads, Pink Panthers, Algerians & Assholes. Everyone was pissed-off from day one. The free spectators on the long hill paralleling the walled concert wanted the wall down—as did the Algerians, who tore down the outer wall during my surreal performance (the noise from this protest was drowned by the noise of those protesting the noise, and by the time it got to the stage, there were half a million people pissed off. Throwing beer cans at the stage.) I said I planned to continue in spite of anything but rifle fire, which I did, exiting after "Bobby McGee" with a middle finger raised to the angry audience, then promoter Ricky Farr (legendary heavyweight Tommy Farr's son) grabbed a mike and cussed out the crowd & the people on the hill & everybody in earshot for about a week. It was something. They hated everybody. Even Jimi, God bless him.

So it's 4 a.m. Sunday morning, end of a death-march, and Zal (Yanofsky) and I stayed around to watch Leonard. The crowd was burning the concession stands & a truck at the time. They woke up Leonard in his trailer, & he appeared in a raincoat & pajamas & took 20 minutes to tune up. They'll kill him, I thought as we watched. They'll never hear him. Then he did the damndest thing you ever saw: he Charmed the Beast. A lone sorrowful voice did what some of the best rockers in the world had tried to do for three days & failed. It really impressed me.

"That's the kind of background I'd like for my songs," I said, admiring the tasty work of Bob Johnston & the boys, & Jennifer Warren.

"Boss," Zal said, "Leonard is an angst poet. You're an alcoholic."

PATRICK LANE

Orpheus

for Leonard Cohen

He is mostly laughter and willingly.
thinking of all those years of music
and the tears given to the wind, struggling

back up through all that silence. a second death
a cruelty he began to understand. To flee
from women. knowing only the trees and stones

could hear his song. This was the mystery
men turned to. a giving up to grief.
a going into song without complaint. for what

else but love had brought him here
to this place of birds and serpents? But to see
such death. and for what? To speak at last

in a voice that touched no one. the women
with their rakes and hoes hacking him to death
for whom the trees let fall their leaves?

And then to have his song lie beached on Lesbos
with Bacchus squatting on his head. cacophony and din
and nothing more? But these are only questions.

He should have known love would bring him this.
and of course the greed of women. their desire.
thinking death a suitable revenge upon neglect.

Orpheus who sang man's mysteries and died for it.
You too who dance upon the beach. you who have never
listened. listen now: the leaves fall without you

and the birds who once sang with you sing alone.
Make your lament. It is only noise.
The whole world does not hear you.

DENNIS LEE

Blue Psalm
(for LC)

Hush hush little
    wanderer. Hush your
    weary load.   Who touched down
once, once, once in America—
    and over you flashed the net!
And they said, You will forget your name and
    your home and
    it was so: already I had forgotten.

But how did I come to be here?
    This place is not my place,
these ways are not my ways.   I
    do not understand their
consumer index: their *life-style options:* their GNP—
    weird abstract superstitions, and
when I settled in to stay,
    it felt unclean.

Son of the house!
For they fed me and
    dressed me in silks, they
    trussed me with first-world pay.
They poured sweet liqueurs on my tongue and said,
    Sing the old ways.
        sing of your roots . . .
    What have I sunk to?

Though they hem me with filigree,
    this is not my country.
Though I bask on a diamond leash it is not my home.
But what am I doing here still, how long will I

      desecrate the name?
who was born to
    another estate, in a
   place I have nearly forgotten.

GILLIAN MCCAIN

Being and Nothingness:
A Homage to Leonard Koan

My first love's band used to do a mind-blowing version of "Famous Blue Raincoat." Grinding guitars and those unforgettable lyrics, "There's music on Clinton Street all through the evening." Clinton Street brought to mind inconceivable beauty—rainy nights, salsa music drifting through open windows, dumptrucks at 4 a.m., too loud for ambient music. A world of possibility.

Eric used to wear a celery-colored shirt that blended into the green walls of my kitchen. It went beautifully with his long hair, the color of a strawberry-carrot blender drink. I used to lean against streetlamps and listen to him busk after the bars closed. The entire downtown of Halifax, Nova Scotia after midnight needed one giant intervention, and I would watch drunks walk by to avoid Eric's cold glances toward me as he played a cover of "So Long, Marianne." I was in love and it had gradually become unrequited. I was trying to cope by pretending that I was only an actress in a kitschy greek tragedy, that these hourly heartbreaks were darkly glamourous. But the crux of my distress wasn't Eric's iciness, but the fact that *I* wanted to be the bard. Leonard once said, "I thought that all women were poets" but in my tiny world, men were the ones who created, women, at best, were the muse. I was the inspiration for a song Eric wrote called "Book of the Dead." I was twenty and my future appeared in front of me like a tight throat with nothing to say. I was destined to be a beautiful loser, a cover model for a remake of "Death of a Ladies' Man."

I left Halifax and moved to New York City, only to discover that a change in environment doesn't change much. Outside my three hours of sleep a night, my days consisted of the oneiric adventures of an insomniac—growing my hair out, not eating, and dressing like an elderly greek woman in mourning, only in tighter garments. I knew I was draining the emotional economy of great nations, of galaxies, but I didn't know what the fuck I was supposed to do about it. There was simply no elbowroom left in the universe. Possibility was impossible.

I continued to listen to Leonard. I got stuck on the lines, "You're living for nothing now / I hope you're keeping some kind of record." Meaninglessness usually precedes action, and I decided that I could use "nothing" as a noose or a bungy cord. I decided on the latter, and allowed nothing to be my muse. Documenting nothing in words became my *raison d'etre*, and I soon discovered that sad but hopeful slice of the world that lives between joy and depression, like the humpback walking calmly up to the stage at the Ritz and placing a small perfectly wrapped gift at Leonard's feet.

I wrote terrible poems for years, and still do a lot of the time, but to this day I'm still obsessed with documenting nothing, which most of the time now feels like something. It's like poet Harris Schiff writes, "a presense where fears says there is none / but there is!" I'm no longer so arrogant as to believe I know what's best for me. "There is a crack in everything / That's how the light gets in" is my secret mantra.

It's been eight years since my Leonard "Koan." Again, I find myself with someone who is obsessed and inspired by Leonard. It's four in the morning, there's music on Bleecker Street, and we're watching the "I'm Your Man" documentary. Liam says, "Leonard Cohen is the only man I would consider turning gay for." I reply, "Leonard Cohen is the only man I would consider marrying on the eve of his sixtieth birthday." We watched the documentary in silence—the tour of his greek bungalow, his three pages a day, his ten-year stopover. Some concert footage comes on with Leonard singing. Liam says, "That is the most beautiful line," and then repeats it. I mishear him and say, "Kissing the jew off your thighs?" We laugh hysterically. We know Leonard would laugh, too.

Leonard, thank you for your modest ecstacy. Happy birthday.

JACK MCCLELLAND

Leonard Cohen

I first met Leonard Cohen through the goodness of our mutual friend Irving Layton. I think in many ways Layton was more than a friend to Leonard, he was a spiritual mentor.

Leonard came to Toronto to my office with the manuscript of what was to become *The Spice Box of Earth.* Although this was many years ago now Leonard was certainly a very impressive young man. At that time I would say that he had a certain aura of shyness about him, as most great actors have; he was certainly confident and self-possessed. There was something about him that gave the impression that he had a promising future, and that was without the support of such a well established poet as Irving Layton. Although I never considered myself an expert or authority on poetry I did break precedence in the case of Leonard Cohen by accepting his first manuscript for publication on the strength of a fast read of a few poems even though our usual procedure involved turning over the manuscript to specialists for review before any publishing decision was reached. That is some indication of how impressive Leonard was as a relatively young man.

I published *Spice Box* in the next twelve months and it received some very promising reviews and it sold well although in relatively small quantities in relation to the Cohen market that ultimately developed.

Leonard and I became acquainted and remained very good friends throughout the years. We met regularly in Montreal, Toronto and in New York and indeed I more than once visited him at his retreat in the Greek islands.

As his career developed he became one of the great entertainers. My daughters became increasingly interested in meeting him and this was easily arranged. Leonard, for many years, has made a practice of sending me tickets when he was performing or going to perform in Toronto and we would meet him after the performance. Quite normally Leonard and I would arrange to have lunch during his visit to Toronto.

Nothing about the foregoing is unique or all that extraordinary given the fact that I was a book publisher and Leonard was to become one of the great singers and entertainers of all time. I retained that relationship despite the fact that I was always honest enough to tell him that although I thought he was a great performer I thought he had a lousy voice. This was not an opinion that my daughters shared.

There's one unique thing about our author-publisher relationship. Leonard did not like the formality of contracts. As a consequence, although we would always send him a contract as a matter of form, inevitably he would not sign and return them. I chose to ignore this. I think over the many years that we published his poetry and his fiction he signed only one contract. With proper foresight on my part I would have realized that this might have dire consequences with the publishing firm in the future because without signed contracts Leonard, in fact, controlled the rights to all his works completely. I'm delighted by the fact that he still publishes with McClelland & Stewart, the company that I sold a few years back and with whom I no longer have any association.

I have been asked many times because of that Layton-Cohen-McClelland connection, how I would compare the two of them as poets. It's not really a problem for me. Layton was THE poet, probably the greatest Canada has ever known. Poetry was his life and his full time dedication. He was, and is Canada's great poet. Having said that I would add I think Leonard Cohen could have written a handful of poems that were better than any achieved by the Master.

DAVID MCFADDEN

Dear Leonard Cohen:
We've never met, but I saw you standing chatting with Margaret Trudeau somewhere in Toronto several years ago. Actually you weren't chatting, you were standing together silently, with angelic smiles on your faces, and both of you seemed to be enveloped in an unearthly white radiance.

I played a tape of yours for a friend, a top-ranking no-nonsense corporate type, who claimed to have never heard your music or read your poems. A few bars into "There Ain't No Cure For Love" my friend burst into tears.

At a book fair in Montreal I met someone who said she was your next-door neighbour. She offered to give you a copy of my book *Gypsy Guitar*. A few weeks later I received a wonderful note from you. It was only a paragraph or two but you said all the right things. You had given the book high-level attention. The letter meant a lot to me.

Leonard Cohen, I see you as an exotic extra-terrestrial who is definitely just visiting. You're a native of an unimaginably strange and remote little planet from which few souls venture forth except on special missions which are inexplicable in human terms. There are many Leonard Cohens on that fortunate planet. On this there is only one.

You are probably the only poet whose work other poets truly *envy*. Your poems, your music, your voice have enriched us for years. Your work baffles us in exactly the way we like to be baffled.

SEYMOUR MAYNE

Two Poems For Leonard

BLESS ME, SAID THE MAN

Bless me, said the man.
Bless you, said the angel
   sneezing at that very moment
   and brushing the man's beard
   with the tremulous ruffle
   of wings.

Again, bless, said the man.
Again, he said
   but there was no answer
   in the other's eyes.

And the man had no choice
   so he blessed himself
as the angel winged his way
   into his mind.

THAT KINGDOM'S ADOPTED SON
for Leonard Cohen

Watching you speak, poet—whispers
in the night . . . thin mists dissolving
in the city's searchlight rays,
and two satellites down in broad daylight.
—No one was amazed. You humped
your shoulders casually; winked, clowned.
You would've wanted your lips
wet with acid, biting; but beige drapes
rose before your eyes over our coffees.
Were you thinking of valleys, looming boulders?
Like that ancient Judean aristocrat,
were your daydreams haunted by fluent
wistful rhythms, skeletal lyres
in tawny hands . . . or slingshots tuned soft?

You leaned on the crook of your arm,
an acute angle spanned by an invisible
silk web. I could swear that with every
motion of your lowered head, your nose
disturbed those elastic threads
like a listless finger on the biblic harp:
Notes of an exile divorced from everyone,
and even from himself, that kingdom's adopted son.

PATRICIA MORLEY

Sitting in the Sun

On a sunny fall day in 1972 I was startled to see Leonard Cohen sitting on the broad, palatial steps of the YM/YWCA on Drummond Street, downtown Montreal. He looked exactly like his photos. Sitting there, he could have passed for a student.

I stopped, introduced myself, and told him that *The Immoral Moralists: Hugh MacLennan and Leonard Cohen* was just out. Leonard smiled. He said he liked "the idea of being in a book with MacLennan." The older novelist had been one of his favorite teachers at McGill.

Leonard looked as if he had all the time in the world, but I was nearly always in a hurry. I went into the Norris Building to teach *The Favorite Game,* and left him sitting in the sun.

SUSAN MUSGRAVE

Leonard and Me

Death of a Lady's Man had just been released. I was in Vancouver
promoting *A Man to Marry, A Man to Bury* and my publicist
invited me to a gathering that evening, in honour of Leonard
Cohen.

We arrived early, and my husband cornered Leonard to tell
him about one of his colleagues at law school, an Adolf Gerloff,
whose mother had given him Cohen's first album for Christ-
mas—not because she loved Cohen's voice, but because Cohen
was a Jewish name and she wanted Adolf to know she could be
open-minded. I left the kitchen and went out on the verandah to
look for the moon.

Secretly, of course, I hoped Leonard would follow. My publi-
cist had told me he admired my poetry, and I imagined him
caressing a dog-eared copy of my first slim volume, and telling
me, "I always read your poetry in bed." But it was more than just
my syntax I hoped he'd get excited about. Taking from his
pocket an old schedule of trains he would look me in the eyes
and say, "Greece would be a good place to look at the moon." I
would lower my needy eyes and tell him I wished to feed him tea
and oranges that came all the way from China, and the next
week Peter Gzowski would be interviewing us about our affair on
national radio. Leonard would say how our visions complemented
one another and I would give an example of finding lines from
one of my poems on a dead friend's bathroom wall: "Is there
really this much desolation / or is it just that I have / found it
all?" paired with a line from one of Leonard's songs, "Then
picking up the pieces that he left behind you would find he did
not leave you very much, not even laughter." Peter would say,
"Where do you go now?" and Leonard would say, "I only read
her poetry in bed."

I watched him coming towards me out of the house, in his
quiet way. He slid in close as if he felt the need to warn me *I told*

117

you when I came I was a stranger. I would have given him head on an unmade bed in the Chelsea Hotel or any other hotel in town when he spoke to me in that voice full of broken whiskey bottles and desire. "I really like your husband," he said.

Death of a ladies man.

Montreal, circa 1979
Photo by Hazel Field

IRA B. NADEL

Leonard and Lorca

*Why struggle with the flesh while the frightening problem of the spirit
exists? I love Venus madly, but even more I love the question, Heart?*
Lorca, May 1918

In 1949 the fifteen year-old Leonard Cohen unexpectedly came
upon a book of poetry in Montreal by Federico García Lorca, a
writer about whom he knew nothing. But since the moment
when he picked up the newly published New Directions volume
of *Selected Poems,* edited by Lorca's younger brother, Francisco
García Lorca, and Donald M. Allen, Cohen has ironically told
the world that Lorca "ruined" his life with his brooding vision
and powerful verse. In print and at concerts, Cohen has re-
peated the lines that first led to the destruction of his purity:
"Through the Arch of Elvira / I want to see you go, / so that I
can learn your name / and break into tears." "Wrap me at dawn
in a veil, / for she will hurl fistfuls of ants" are two additional
lines recalled from the same source, "The Divan at Tamarit" (CP
681, 665). Lorca was, and remains, a seminal influence on Cohen;
as poet, performer, and artist, Lorca—quite literally killed by
twentieth century politics when executed by Granadan Falangists
on 19 August 1936 shortly after his return to Spain to aid in the
Civil War—stands as the first of a series of representative artists
for Cohen. Louis Dudek, F.R. Scott. A.M. Klein and Irving Layton
would follow, but Lorca was his premier poetic model.

Lorca's life and Cohen's are strangely parallel. Son of a well-
to-do landowning family from Granada, Lorca found formal study
at, first, Granada University and then the celebrated Residencia
de Estudiantes in Madrid, tedious and spent most of his energy
on avant-garde cultural life. Like Cohen at McGill, Lorca's aca-
demic performance was desultory, hardly bothering to sit exami-
nations after his first year. Lorca concentrated on developing his
talent as a pianist, composing as well as performing. In fact, one

of his early disappointments was his parents' failure to allow him to move to Paris to continue his musical studies in 1916; Lorca, with seeming casualness, then "'turned his creative urges to poetry'" as he wrote in a 1929 autobiographical note (G 47). At university and La Residencia, however, Lorca made several lifelong friends: Guillermo de Torre, who would edit his work, the poet Jose Bergamin, and Salvador Dali. At the University of Granada, Lorca read law and took his degree for the sake of a title and to please his father, but concentrated on piano and guitar study, developing a friendship with the great composer Manuel de Falla. During this time he also collected, arranged and performed Spanish folk songs and he would later often accompany his poems with either a piano or guitar.

Cohen's time at McGill (1951-55) was similar, from his brief attempt at law under the direction of F.R. Scott to his performing poetry with musical accompaniment at Stanley Street coffee houses and Dunn's Jazz Parlor. And he, too, made lifelong friends at university, among them F.R. Scott, Irving Layton and Morton Rosengarten. During their university years, both writers seriously undertook the promotion of their literary careers. And as Cohen would do in 1956, Lorca went to New York in 1929 to attend Columbia University, as well as to travel and write. From John Jay Hall at Columbia in November 1929, Lorca reports to Carlos Morla Lynch that "I have five classes and spend the day greatly amused as if in a dream," a comment equally apt for Cohen during his time in the General Studies program (SL 152). Yet for Lorca, this was a period of extraordinary productivity: *Poeta en Nueva York, Yerma, Asi que pasen cinco años*, and a filmscript *Viaje a la luna* were all written at this time. A trip to Havana in the spring of 1930 from New York, before his return to Spain, and a 1933 trip to Buenos Aires, highlight the peripatetic nature of Lorca shared by Cohen who would also visit Cuba, just days before the Bay of Pigs invasion in April 1961.

Lorca's own fanciful belief that he possessed the blood of gypsies and Jews enhanced Cohen's identification with him while his elegiac tone, faith in a spiritual absolute and struggle between the artist and society echo throughout the work of Cohen.

And three questions by Lorca clearly anticipate themes that animate Cohen's writing:

> Am I to blame for being a Romantic and a dreamer in a life that is all materialism and stupidity? Am I to blame for having a heart, and for having been born among people interested only in comfort and in money? What stigma has passion placed on my brow? (CP xxv)

Similar questions absorb Cohen who constantly offers answers and demonstrations of their centrality for him. And not surprisingly for romantics like Lorca and Cohen, they idealize women, especially those that inspire. To a young woman in 1918 Lorca wrote "there are times . . . when we feel the desire to write to a soul unseen far off in the distance and that that soul hear our call of friendship. . . . " "Perhaps," he tells her, "you are, like me, a romantic who dreams of something very spiritual, that you cannot find" (SL 1). Impassioned, he tells the woman she is one who advances "along the road of life leaving a wake of tranquility, of sympathy, of spiritual calm. Something like the perfume of a flower hidden away in the distance." Cohen in "Beneath My Hands" or "I Long to Hold Some Lady" expresses the same sincere attitude clearly expressed in "The Reason I Write": "The reason I write / is to make something / as beautiful as you are," a view of women comically echoed in "My Room" or "MARITA": "MARITA / PLEASE FIND ME / I AM ALMOST 30" (SM 119, 173, 116). A celebration of the feminine through poetry provides each poet with energy and power: "Ripe with lost poems, / I step naked into the street" Lorca exuberantly writes (CP 43).

Other parallels between Lorca and Cohen include their absorption with music. Not only did both compose and absorb musical elements in their verse techniques, but they each used music as a subject for their poems. *Poem of the Deep Song* (1921-22) is a major experimental work by Lorca employing such musical forms as ballads, suites and capriccios; song, instruments and dance comprise its subject matter. Dialogues, dramatized encounters by isolated voices, much like Cohen's closet drama

121

"The New Step" also appear. Lorca described the rhythm of *Poem of the Deep Song* as "popular in a stylized way" that brings out "all the old *cantaores.*" Cohen's use of music as a subject is seen in poems like "When I Hear You Sing" or "Calm, Alone, the Cedar Guitar" and, of course, in songs like "A Singer Must Die" and "Tower of Song." The nature, and at times impossibility, of music is a constant issue for Cohen as he yearns for that "secret chord / that David played to please the Lord" and "even though it all went wrong, / I'll stand before the Lord of Song / with nothing on my lips but Hallelujah!" (SM 347). Similarly, both Lorca and Cohen display an interest in drawing, Lorca often filling his letters with images and occasionally illustrating his poems. He also had a wonderful habit of visually enhancing photographs as a self-portrait from 1927 records; extending his feet is the base of a Roman column while ballooning from his mouth is a cartoon statement. Cohen has also illustrated several poems and painted a great deal, occasionally offering that art for sale and reproducing it in his concert programs.

Lorca and Cohen equally possess a fascination with film. In New York, Lorca worked on a surrealistically oriented filmscript, *Trip to the Moon*, conceived for the silent cinema; Dali's and Bunuel's *Un Chien andalou* ("An Andalusian dog") may, in fact, be partly based on Lorca. Cohen has on several occasions sought to write filmscripts, especially of his novels. He has also regularly participated in films, from Donald Brittain's NFB documentary of 1964, to the 1966 short *Angel*, the 1967 film *Poem* based on his reading a passage from *Beautiful Losers*, his 1972 project *Bird on a Wire*, and his 1984 video, *I am a Hotel.* The use of cinematic techniques in *Beautiful Losers* is another sign of the importance of film for his writing.

Additionally, two unique cities absorbed each writer: Granada and Montreal. Indeed, what Granada meant to Lorca, Montreal has meant to Cohen, combining an aesthetic idea with an image of his own sexuality and poetry. Montreal, "a poem factory" for Cohen as he announced in *The Favorite Game*, finds a parallel in Lorca's response to Granada: "All day I turn out poems like a factory" he wrote in September 1928 (SL 139). But each city also ironically confirmed a melancholy certainty that life seemed spatially and temporally "elsewhere." Hence, their constant travel.

In their work, Granada and Montreal became images of elegy and absence, something to be admired and yet rejected, a condition poetically captured by Lorca:

> It [Granada] is an astounding wealth. A wealth that stylizes everything, and where nothing can be captured . . . . It is not pictorial, just as a river is not architectural. Everything flows, plays and escapes. It is poetic, musical. A city of fugues without a skeleton. Melancholy with vertebrae. That is why I can't live here. (CP xii)

Not surprisingly, both writers leave and yet return to their centers.

Aesthetically joining the work of Lorca and Cohen is, first, an emotionalism released through art; "in my soul," Lorca explains, "is a forest full of nests which come to life with the breeze of my great passion" (SL 10). Cohen echoes this condition throughout the confessional quality of his verse and song, displaying the nakedness of self generated by passion and feeling. " I want me to be myself" Lorca further declared, adding "I only know . . . that my heart . . . has huge, impossible desires," a proclamation equally valid for Cohen (SL 3; CP xxv). Formally, traditional rather than avant-garde verse forms attract the two writers. Parallelism, repetition, and refrains are key features of both poets, as well as the expressive manipulation of verb tenses. Of greatest importance is their shared sense of the musical nature of poetry: "a ballad," wrote Lorca, "is not perfect unless it has its own melody to make it palpitate and give it blood and a severe or erotic air for its characters to move around in" (CP xlvi). Narrative poetry that "lives in variants", or mystery, sustains the enigma that is fundamental to Lorca and Cohen's writing. Gaps or narrative fragmentation are part of the story and, as Lorca lucidly explained in an essay concerning the narrative dimension of the ballad, "I wanted to fuse the narrative ballad with the lyrical without affecting the quality of either" (CP xlix). This ideal is perhaps what Cohen seeks in his poetic songs and lyrical poetry.

In addition, visual detail often replaces narrative explanation, a feature Cohen fully explores in texts like "The Failure of a Secular Life," or "When Even The" (SM 56, 388).

Furthermore, in Lorca's prose poems, works such as "Submerged Swimmer" (1928), one discovers the origin of many of Cohen's own images and forms. "We argued. I scratched my forehead, and she very skillfully split the glass surface of her cheek. Then we embraced," Lorca states in the work (CP 613). Here, the surrealist blend of the domestic with the violent prefigures scenes and language found in Cohen; "The Music Crept By Us" and "You have No Form" are two examples (SM 58, 255). "A Sense of the Morning" from *Death of a Lady's Man*, clarifies this approach: "You are at the centre of your world. We are trying to circumcise your heart. But you cannot stop me from screaming. Yes, we have muffled your voice. You must, you must. This leaves us with a sense of the morning" (DLM 68). "I get up to love and eat and kill, not by my own, but by our married will" Cohen later writes, sarcastically adding, "*They should cast your cunt in chrome for the radiator cap of a Buick*" to intensify yet objectify his anger (DLM 100).

The frequent use of the prose poem by Cohen finds its origin again in Lorca who developed the form in "Suicide in Alexandria" and "Two Lovers Murdered by a Partridge." The former contains a wonderful Cohen-like passage: "Now there's no solution. Kiss me, but don't wreck my tie. Kiss me, kiss me" (CP 615). Cohen experimented with the prose poem as early as "Friends" in his first book, *Let Us Compare Mythologies* (1956), and continued with "Lines from My Grandfather's Journal" in *The Spice-Box of Earth* (1961). In *Death of a Lady's Man* (1977) he extended the form while exploring it fully in the prose psalms that make up *Book of Mercy* (1984). In Lorca he also found dialogs such as "Dialogue of Amargo, the Bitter One" which may have been the inspiration for such works as "The New Step" or "The Project."

Yet, it is traditional forms of verse, whether the Golden Age of Spanish poetry for Lorca or the English Romantics for Cohen, that hold sway. Lorca and Cohen did not have the so-called *antipassatismo* required to sustain experimental writing. What they

124

possess, instead, is a deep Romanticism strikingly expressed by Lorca in a letter written to the Futurist poet Adriano del Valle in 1918:

> I am a great Romantic and this is my greatest pride. In a century of zeppelins and of stupid deaths, I sit at my piano and weep as I dream of the mist of Handel, and I write verses that are very much my *own*, singing the same way to Christ as to Buddha, to Mohammed as to Pan. (CP xxiv)

Allowing for historical change, Leonard Cohen could have just as easily written these two sentences. Furthermore, while there is a strong anti-bourgeois feeling in Lorca and Cohen, neither display the nihilism or radical subversion of language found in Dadaism or Surrealism. Neither is antagonistic toward the public but consciously sought wide and diverse audiences, Lorca thrilling to his reception in Havana, for example, when he read there in the Spring of 1930 or Buenos Aires in 1933. Cohen, similarly, finds great satisfaction in his admiring audiences, offering repeated encores to his often exuberant listeners. As early as 1964, the rapport between Cohen and his audience was evident: witness their reaction to his comic narration of a visit to a friend in a Montreal mental hospital in Donald Brittain's NFB film. As recently as June 1993, during his Vancouver concert, he displayed a similar ease and skill at repartee. At the third interruption by an ardent female who, when he introduced the line "Let's do something crazy" from "Waiting for the Miracle," screamed "Yesss! Leonard," Cohen seductively whispered so all could hear, "There is nothing like an idea whose force does not diminish with repetition"—to the great delight of his audience.

Explaining the sadness and sorrow that often suffuses Cohen's work is an elegiac sense of experience found in Lorca's work. In its contrast of presence and absence, the elegy is the form that contains desire to have what is absent or does not exist. Or as Lorca wrote in a work that greatly appealed to Cohen, "Divan del Tamarit" ("The Divan at Tamarit"), "I am the enormous shadow of my tears." The poem, itself, is a substitute for the desired but

125

absent object, as many of the poems in *The Energy of Slaves* and *Death of a Lady's Man* make clear.

"The Divan at Tamarit" is a collection of twenty compositions written by Lorca between 1931 and 1934, although it was not published until 1940. *Divan* in Spanish derives from the Persian *diwan*, one of whose meanings is a collection of poetry, especially in Arabic. *Tamarit* is an Arabic proper name referring to a country house of Lorca's uncle outside of Granada; it means "abundant in dates." "Ghazals" designate the eleven poems in section one, short compositions associated with Persian lyric poetry connected with music and designed to be sung. They also deal with an erotic or amorous subject. Written in distichs, the first two lines rhyme in consonance with the rhyme and then continue in the even lines throughout the poem. Usually, the poet names himself at the end of the poem. The nine "Qasidas" that form the next collection in the work are poems longer than any previous type in Arabic poetry with a certain internal architecture developing a single rhyme and metre throughout with a minimum of thirty lines. The form was an established genre in pre-Islamic Arabic poetry.

A closer reading of Lorca's "Divan", however, shows how little formal similarity exists between them and classical Arab verse. Rather, they embody the voice of Lorca and his personal concerns: death, lost love and the metaphysical problems of life in which love and death are complexly assimilated—themes frequently and tragically repeated in Cohen's poetry, whether in the early poems from his first book, "Ballad," and "Lovers," or more wittily expressed in his recent song, "Closing Time":

> And I miss you since the place got wrecked
> by the winds of change and the weeds of sex
> looks like freedom but it feels like death
> it's something in between, I guess
> it's closing time. (SM 379)

The opening text of "Divan", "Ghazal of Love Unforeseen," with its themes of love expressed through language, exhibits the

126

appeal of Lorca's writing for Cohen through its juxtaposition of unexpected images:

No one understood the perfume, ever:
the dark magnolia of your belly.
No one ever knew you martyred
love's hummingbird between your teeth.

"I searched my breast to give you / the ivory letters saying: Ever" the narrator adds at the close of the penultimate stanza and concludes the poem with an image ennobling the death of the speaker in the blood of the loved one:

Ever, ever, my agony's garden,
your elusive form forever:
blood of your veins in my mouth,
your mouth now lightless for my death. (CP 655)

The dark and surrealistic quality of the poetry strongly influenced Cohen's imagery and tone as in "The Poems Don't Love Us Anymore" or the poem "The Death of A Lady's Man" (SM 186, 227).

Lorca's influence has extended to the very conception of new works for Cohen. His 1988 recording of Lorca's poem "Little Viennese Waltz" as his song "Take This Waltz" is a primary example, with Cohen's vision of song not far from Lorca's. "What I am trying to do," Lorca explained,

is to get at the dramatic depths of the ballad, and set them into action. First of all, assign each line of verse to the proper voice, and then suggest the atmosphere [of the poem] with lovely figures. This is an extremely stylized evocation, with only the faintest indication of the action.

Such an evocation, he adds, "ought to be based on slow movements and motionless faces . . . it ought to be the plastic algebra of a drama of passion and pain" (CP xl). The phrase "plastic

127

algebra" is pure Cohen.

Lorca's poem appears in Section IX of *Poet in New York*, titled "Flight from New York (Two Waltzes toward Civilization)." First published in 1934, the poem and its companion, "Waltz in the Branches," were to have formed part of a book Lorca was planning in 1933 entitled *Because I Love Only You (Set of Waltzes)*. The book was to be written in "'Waltz time . . . like this, sweet, lovable, vaporous'" (PNY 275). by 1934 the poem was incorporated into *Poet in New York*, then known as *Introduction to Death*. In a 1988 CBC documentary, Cohen showed the host, Adrienne Clarkson, pages and pages of verse translations of Lorca's poem indicating his labor over the shift from Spanish to English which, when distilled, became the words of his song. A comparison of the first stanza of each illustrates his method of structural and tonal ambivalence as he switches between major and minor modes, stated most clearly in the musical notation, but suggested by the language alone. Interestingly, one hears lines grouped as quatrains, although on the album *I'm Your Man* (1988) they are printed as paragraphs; in *Stranger Music*, however, they appear as verse (353). Lorca begins "Little Viennese Waltz" with

> In Vienna there are ten little girls,
> a shoulder for death to cry on,
> and a forest of dried pigeons.
> There is a fragment of tomorrow
> in the museum of winter frost.
> There is a thousand-windowed dance hall.
>
> *Ay, ay, ay, ay!*
> Take this close-mouthed waltz.
>
> Little waltz, little waltz,
> of itself, of death, and of brandy
> that dips its tail in the sea. (PNY 167)

Cohen reorders, poeticizes and dramatizes this into:

Now in Vienna there are ten pretty women. There's a shoulder where Death comes to cry. There's a lobby with nine-hundred windows. There's a tree where the doves go to die. There's a piece that was torn from the morning, and it hangs in the Gallery of Frost. Ay, Ay, Ay, Ay. Take this waltz, take this waltz, take this waltz with the clamp on its jaws.

Expanding the images and adding a stronger surrealistic element to the original, Cohen, of course, augments the verse with the addition of music. The poem as song becomes a metacommentary on the deathly tradition it possesses which the refrain clarifies: "This waltz, this waltz, this waltz, this waltz. With its very own breath of brandy and Death. Dragging its tail in the sea." Cohen in his song musically explores the limitations of the waltz through the re-membering of Lorca's poem and the exploration of its conventions via the interplay of the text and its tone which, remember, is sung. Appropriating conventions, Cohen creates a stylized waltz, exaggerating the musicality of the form, reclaiming, not rejecting, Lorca's original expression.

Lorca's transcendental vision "'taught me that poetry can be pure and profound, and at the same time popular'" Cohen reported to a Spanish journalist (D 37). He also identified with Lorca's surrealism, as well as his qualified use of dreams as a technique. Lines from "The King of Harlem," written by Lorca in 1929, represent the appeal. One verse reads

Oblivion was expressed by three drops of ink on the monocle.
Love by a single, invisible, stone-deep face.
And above the clouds, bone marrow and corollas
composed a desert of stems without a single rose. (PNY 35)

Cohen understood the value of mixing images and the beauty that can be generated from the comparison of simple objects as two marvelous lines from Lorca's poem "St. Michael" demonstrate: "The sea is dancing on the beach / a poem of balconies" (CP 541). "We Latins" explained Lorca, "want sharp profiles and visible mystery. Form and sensuality" (PNY xvii). The statement, found in Lorca's 1928 lecture "Imagination, Inspiration, Evasion," represents equally well Cohen's aesthetic. And Cohen's naming his daughter Lorca attests to the presiding presence of García Lorca in his life.

Leonard Cohen seriously began to write his own poetry in 1950 at sixteen (Lorca was seventeen); it occurred a year after he read Lorca's *Selected Poems*, "sitting down at a card table on a sun porch one day when I decided to quit a job. I was working in a brass foundry [of his uncle Lawrence's, called W.R. Cuthbert] at the time and one morning I thought, I just can't take this any more, and I went out to the sun porch and I started a poem. I had a marvelous sense of mastery and power, and freedom, and strength, when I was writing this poem" (SN [1969]; see *Favorite Game* Bk. 2 Ch. 15 for ref. to the foundry). Lorca's early experiences were similar—finding poetry a way of responding to the history and beauty of Andalusia. And immediately evident in his early work was a rebellion against Catholicism and a sexual malaise, not unlike Cohen's treatment of religion and sexuality in his first book, *Let Us Compare Mythologies* (which like Lorca's first book, *Impressions and Landscapes* [1918] was self-financed). Sexual love was the obsession of both young poets who found Dionysius more appealing than Apollo.

Anticipating the formative influence of Lorca on Cohen was that of Ruben Dario on Lorca who first read the Nicaraguan poet at nineteen. In his refined eroticism, *fin-de-siecle* themes and musicality, Dario became a significant model for the youthful Lorca, not only poetically, but in his admiration for America expressed in Dario's "To Roosevelt" and in his sonnet on Whitman. The impact of Dario and his *modernismo* on Lorca is equal to that of Lorca's on Cohen. Through his lyricism, romanticism and surrealism, plus his experimentation with form and incorporation of suffering and music into his verse, Lorca demonstrated the possibilities of poetry that contains but is not overrun by sadness:

There is an ache in the flesh of my heart,
in the flesh of my soul.

And when I speak
my words bob in the air
like corks on water. (CP xxix)

Lorca was clearly Cohen's first and foremost poetic author-
ity—and, one is tempted to write, most lasting.

Works Cited

Cohen, Leonard. *Death of A Lady's Man.* Toronto: McClelland and
Stewart, 1978. DLM.

—. *Stranger Music: Selected Poems and Songs.* Toronto: McClelland and
Stewart, 1993. SM.

Dorman, L.S. and C.L. Rawlins. *Leonard Cohen: Prophet of the Heart.*
London: Omnibus, 1990. D.

Gibson, Ian. *Federico García Lorca, A Life.* NY: Pantheon, 1989. G.

Harris, Michael. Leonard Cohen: The Poet as Hero 2," Saturday Night
June 1969. 26-30. SN.

Lorca, Federico García, *Collected Poems.* ed. Christopher Maurer. tr.
Francisco Aragon, et al. NY: Farrar Straus Giroux, 1991. CP.

—. *Poet in New York.* ed. Christopher Maurer; tr. Greg Simon and
Steven F. White. NY: Noonday Press, 1988. PNY.

—. *Selected Letters.* ed. & tr. David Gershator. NY: New Directions, 1983.
SL.

JOHN NEWLOVE

Two Poems for Leonard Cohen

LEONARD, IT'S WINTER IN OTTAWA

The streets are full of overweight corporals,
of sad grey computer captains, the impedimenta
of a capital city, struggling through the snow.

There is cold gel on my belly, an instrument
is stroking it incisively, the machine
in the half-lit room is scribbling my future.

It is not illegal to be unhappy.
A shadowy technician says alternately,
Breathe, and, You may stop now.
It is not illegal to be unhappy.

THE CAT

It is not epiphanies we are after
God forbid!
but a small truth or two—

—the vinegar lakes, the excremental rivers,
  the cancer fish, the grey-haired trees, the coughing birds
at their song
all summer long,
  the place manipulating the people—

the world makes us what we want
the world makes us want.

The cat
slouches off, out of the poem, sure of itself,
bored.
We make the world.

KEN NORRIS

This Poet Ruined My Life

It was the amazing summer of 1968. I was seventeen, riding the Long Island Railroad out to Stony Brook for freshman orientation. At the train station I'd just bought a copy of *Selected Poems 1956-68*.

I found many of the early poems compelling, but the one that truly did me in was "Owning Everything." It welcomed me into a world I just had to inhabit. It made me want to dedicate my life to poetry. It prompted me to eventually head north to check out the Christ-haunted city of Montreal.

There's no doubt about it: this poet ruined my life. Thanks, Leonard.

P.K. PAGE

Inebriate

During the day I laugh and during the night I sleep.
My favorite cooks prepare my meals,
my body cleans and repairs itself,
and all my work goes well.
  "I Have Not Lingered in European Monasteries"
                                    —Leonard Cohen

Here is eternity as we dream it—perfect.
Another dimension. Here the ship of state
has sprung no leaks, the captain doesn't lie.
The days are perfect and each perfect minute
extends itself forever at my wish.
Unending sunlight falls upon the steep
slope of the hillside where the children play.
And I am beautiful. I know my worth
and when I smile I show my perfect teeth.
During the day I laugh and during the night I sleep.

A dreamless, healing sleep. I waken
to everlasting Greece as white and blue
as music in my head—
an innocent music.
I had forgotten such innocence exists,
forgotten how it feels
to live with neither calendars nor clocks.
I had forgotten how to un-me myself.
Now, as I practise how and my psyche heals
my favorite cooks prepare my meals.

I am not without appetite, nor am I greedy.
My needs are as undemanding as my tastes:
spring water, olives, cucumber and figs

135

and a small fish on a white plate.
To lift my heart I have no wish for wine—
the sparkling air is my aperitif.
Like Emily I am inebriate.
Rude health is mine—and privilege. I bathe
in sacred waters of the river Alph.
My body cleans and repairs itself.

Poised between Earth and Heaven, here I stand
proportions perfect—outspread arms and legs
within a circle—Leonardo's man.
So do I see the giddy Cosmos. Stars
beyond stars unfold for me and shine.
My telephoto lens makes visible
time future and time past, and timeless time
receives me like its child. I am become
as intricate and simple as a cell
and all my work goes well.

AL PURDY

Leonardo

It was 1960, more or less. Milton Acorn and I went to see Leonard Cohen at his pad in Montreal. Acorn was at that time the best poet in Canada. He looked like a fire hydrant that had been pissed on for centuries. And he wrote like an angel.

Leonard Cohen—everybody knows who Leonard Cohen is if they live on this planet or any of the ones nearby. Milton Acorn is dead.

Cohen impressed me then as an aristocrat. Not the kind riding in that rattling cart to the French guillotine, but an aristocrat nevertheless. Acorn then and thereafter was a Communist. The encounter between them ought to have been memorable, but I can remember very little about it except the contrast between the two men. Conversation was, of course, about politics. And Cohen said: "Milton, if Communism is ever outlawed in Canada, and the Mounties round up all subversives, you'd be among the first arrested."

Not true. Acorn was much too obvious a Communist, and like me could never keep his mouth shut. The Mounties would grin and ask him for his autograph.

And another time at Frank Scott's place in Westmount. Scott was a sort of den mother to writers; a law prof, he fought Premier Duplessis in the courts and won. Cohen had recommended Bob Dylan to Scott, the latter rushing out to buy a couple of records. Then a dozen of us listened to Dylan, lounging around on sofas and carpet, imbibing culture.

I couldn't stand it. Dylan sounded to me as if he had a bad cold, pneumonia in the offing. I retired to the kitchen where Marian (Frank's wife) kept the beer.

Well, I admire Cohen a great deal. Having no voice whatever, his voice sounds great. A bit like Margaret Atwood, I've always thought. When I first heard him sing "Suzanne" by the river in Montreal, girls passed out a mile away from where his voice was decibelling.

A later memory is meeting Leonard at "The Night of a Hundred Authors" in Toronto. He was moaning that no one had told him he was supposed to wear dinner clothes. I said it wouldn't have mattered if he was *au naturel*, only his writing was important.

But that's likely wrong. When you're a cult figure, your personality is important as well. (I'm lucky: I don't have one.) However, I still believe Cohen's writing is more important than his music, will survive his personality and his death. For how long? Until language itself changes in the radioactive future.

Harry Rasky and Leonard Cohen
Photo by Hazel Field

HARRY RASKY

The Song of Leonard Cohen

Like a bird on a wire
Like a drunk in an old midnight choir
I have tried in my way to be free

I don't know about being a bird on a wire or being like a drunk
in an old midnight choir, but my pal Leonard, in his own way,
has certainly tried to be free. And as the world turns, he has been
doing a damn fine job of it. Getting better and more free all the
time.

When I first met Leonard he was a poet, of course. Probably
he was born that. But he had yet to add the music. The year was
1961. It was on the island of Hydra, half a day by cruise ship from
Athens. I was on my way back from filming in Ethiopia and had
to wash Addis Abbaba right out of my hair. I had not meant to
stay despite the glaring beauty of the island built on a cliff. But I
was told there was a fellow Canadian living there. We met down
by the docks and the retsina wine and ouzo flowed freely and
Leonard suggested I might like to just hang out for a few days.
He was then, as now, very persuasive. Daily, the guide from the
cruise boat would come by and ask if I was ready to return to
routine and the mainland. But the life was too friendly and free.
Poets don't have it so bad I thought. Just as long as they never
have to go home.

Each night there was the bazouki music. The dancing and the
Greek night air. So soothing. And so much time to talk of dreams.
For Leonard, this meant the long night of dreaming of being a
major published poet. The music was yet to come.

When I left the magical island, Leonard and his friends were
left on the dockside holding onto their chairs because I had this
theory that I was so egocentric that the rest of the world disap-
peared if I was not there to be a part of it. But we vowed that
someday we would find a way of working together.

I can say that in the years that have followed I have come to love Leonard. He is a man to love.

Twenty years were to pass before I was to make my film, *The Song of Leonard Cohen*. In that time I had seen Leonard in New York where I was then living and he was giving serious thought to trying to work at Time or some regular job. I reminded him that he was trying to be free.

We met in many places, many times, including on a Buddhist retreat on top of Mount Baldy. We became seekers of soul together.

And I returned to Hydra and the island I came to love with an early romance. By then the music had come and Leonard would never be an unknown poet on a quiet sun-baked island alone again.

The legend of Leonard was spreading. Women adored him. Of all ages. They still do.

By the time the film was made, Leonard was in and out of a strange interlude, an ill-conceived marriage. He had just completed *Death of a Ladies' Man*. He was feeling down, hurt, like a song gone wrong.

But the love in the man was so great, the words grew stronger. The music richer. He had begun to mix the Hebraic melodies with the poetry of Persia. He was becoming the universal poet. Not bound by any landmass or time. His life was becoming a metaphor for everyone who was striving to make a spiritual and emotional connection.

The film followed him on a journey through half a dozen countries. It is a banquet, a feast of Cohen. It is a festival of friendship. Our lives are bound by it.

The Song of Leonard Cohen has tried in its way to make us all free.

STEPHEN SCOBIE

"This is for Leonard, if he's still here"—Bob Dylan, 1975

When the house-lights go down
in that moment of darkness

    he steps onto the stage
    he creates his own light

we can call him Len or Lennie now
or like the desk-clerk at the Chelsea Hotel
we can call him "Mr Cohen"

    but Leonard is standing
    still in the wings
    watching as "Leonard Cohen"
    steps into the spotlight

and makes a gracious speech
to the audience's applause

strikes up the band, Julie and Perla
hands by their sides, demure in black

their voices as sweet as a lost twin ghost
dancing in the haunted house of love

    Len or Lennie in the spotlight
    graceful, dis-gracing himself

    the dark suit
    the dark voice

from the front row a woman is leaning
leaning out for love, she will

hold that rose forever

    Leonard is standing
    still in the wings, watching
    this other person
    perform his songs

    all the words are memorised
    he is singing along with himself
    every night, this repeated
    karaoke of the spirit

until the applause
breaks over him like a wall
collapsing in an avalanche

    and he stands there awkwardly
    holding the microphone
    wondering what happened to Leonard Cohen

    wondering about this light, where it comes from
    where it's going.

WINFRIED SIEMERLING

Leonard Cohen. "Loneliness and History: A Speech Before the Jewish Public Library"

Montreal 1964. Manuscript Collection 122, "Leonard Cohen Papers," Thomas Fisher Rare Book Library, University of Toronto, Box 9.

INTRODUCTION

"Loneliness and History: A Speech Before the Jewish Public Library" is the title inscribed on a folder that is part of the "Leonard Cohen Papers" at the University of Toronto. The words "Montreal 1964" have been added later.[1] The manuscript pages and notes contained in this folder are of interest for a number of reasons. Cohen comments here, for instance, on A.M. Klein and his role for other Jewish writers at the time. Against this background, Cohen also explains some of the assumptions about poetic speech and the position of the poet with respect to audience and community that seemed important to him during that period. As Birk Sproxton noted in his response to the papers presented at the 1993 Cohen conference in Red Deer, Alberta, the year 1964 "emerges as a critical point in Cohen's career."[2] Eli Mandel looked at the same year when he remarked in 1977 that (what he called at the time) "Cohen's later work, beginning with *Flowers for Hitler* and his songs, develops a murderously ambiguous seduction/repulsion pattern" that is mediated by the mode of address,[3] and pointed to the importance of the context of history here and in *Beautiful Losers* (which was written in 1964 and pub-

---

[1] While the Jewish Public Library does not have any tape recordings of the speech, Cohen himself confirmed in a 1990 interview (see p. 156) that the year is probably correct.

[2] "Reading Leonard Cohen: Reprise." *Canadian Poetry* 33 (Fall/Winter 1993), 124.

[3] "Cohen's Life as a Slave," *Another Time* (Erin, Ont.: Porcepic, 1977), 126.

lished two years later). Cohen's reflections in "Loneliness and History" seem particularly relevant in this context.[4] On the one hand, they develop a notion of history as function of a communicative situation; on the other hand, they suggest links between loneliness, poetic speech, and address. The term loneliness is strikingly used in this manuscript in two opposed senses, whose interplay produces an intriguing dialectic. At times the traditional aspect of alienation is assumed, usually in the sense of a separation from nature and creation (as for instance also in a passage of *Beautiful Losers* in which the Iroquois who "gathered at the priest's hem shivered with a new kind of loneliness."[5]) Other passages, however, can be read profitably in the context of such essays as Emerson's "Self-Reliance" or "Nature." Here, as in the title's emphasis, loneliness appears in the context of intellectual independence and as a point of privileged access to creation. Commenting in particular on the relationship between the outsider poet/prophet and community, Cohen remarked in an interview in 1990 (see pages 154-169 of this volume) that, while he "was stimulated by those ideas in those days," other perspectives became important later. But while Cohen suggests here that an "older writer has different pressing concerns" (and points to "Tower of Song" in this context), he simultaneously acknowledges that the issues that come to the fore in "Loneliness and History" "are legitimate and urgent concerns of a young writer."— W.S.

[4.] I provide a longer discussion of "Loneliness and History in *Discoveries of the Other: Alterity in the Work of Leonard Cohen, Hubert Aquin, Michael Ondaatje, and Nicole Brossard* (Toronto: University of Toronto Press, 1994)

[5.] (Toronto: McClelland and Stewart, 1966), 87.

The manuscript consists of three different parts, one in Roman numerals from I to III (listed here as "A"), one paginated in Arabic numerals from 1 to 6 (listed here as "B"), and one in letters from a-f (with the letter e used twice; listed as "C"); one page, which may have been part of an alternative introduction, is not marked (listed as "D").

[A. Three pages, marked I-III:]

I

The Book Club[a]

The Traitor

The human race needs more traitors.

But when he called me traitor he meant that I had joined another side. If he had read the book he would know that there are no sides for me.

I have lived outside of any [illegible word] community

I know nothing about Talmud.

b

I have no statistics[c] on the community. It will survive, I hope.[d] The terms may be different. In Montreal we have always thought of ourselves as a community in the American sense, + our problems were preserving our identity in the Melting Pot. There are possible, even likely changes, in the [illegible word] situation. We might find ourselves

II

a minority, not in a melting pot situation, but in a very European situation. Again we will be Jews in the midst of a homoge-

---

[a][Inserted on top and in right margin:] I am afraid I am going to talk about myself. All my best friends are Jews but I am the only Jew I know really well.

[b][Inserted between lines, first word circled:] Yiddish - I would have liked to speak in Y.)

[c][Inserted between lines:] your writers - I wonder if any language

[d][Inserted between lines:] but I dare not speak of survival. There are too many big numbers in the air, too much sad confetti fall from the trains

neous nation with their own national culture and religion. A European predicament which I believe we are not at all prepared to encounter.

Perhaps we can discuss this later.
a

The only thing I can do, indeed must do, is make some kind of personal statement. I do not regard a speech before people as a casual luxury, that is why I prefer to read poems which I have worked on. I do not like to waste collective time.[b]

So I have tried to prepare a personal statement for tonight.[c]

III

I have been influenced by a remark of Emerson's. It is this. 'What you are, speaks so loudly that I cannot hear you, that is, Reality speaks so loudly in you that I can't hear what you are saying.

I ask you to apply this insight to me. I shall apply it to you. I will always feel what you are more deeply than what you say.

[B. Six pages marked 1-6:]

1

Traitor[d]

Priest and prophet

Loneliness - Montreal

Silence

God

I remember AM Klein speaking,[e] whose poems disturbed me

---

[a][Crossed out]: I cannot speak before you

[b][Illegible phrase inserted]

[c][Crossed out:] It deals with ideas which are of great concern to me at the moment.

[d][Inserted on top and in the right margin:] 'What you are, speaks so loudly I cannot hear what you say—Reality speaks so loudly in you I can't hear what you are saying to distract me from it

[e][Inserted in right margin and between lines:]—an affidavit from God. AM Klein)

because at certain crucial moments in them he used the word 'we' instead of the word 'I'

because he spoke with too much responsibility, he was too much a champion of the cause, too much the theorist of the Jewish party line

but when he is true to his terror, then he sings, when he begs God to keep 'the golden dome'[a] his mind safe from disease, offering as sacrificial payment his limbs, his body's health - then he sings out of the terror which makes a man lively and comfortless

2

and sometimes his nostalgia for a warm, rich past becomes more than nostalgia, becomes, rather, an impossible longing, an absolute and ruthless longing for the presence of the devine [sic], for the evidence of holiness. Then he is alone and I believe him. Then there is no room for the "we" and if I want to join him, if, even, I want to greet him, I must make my own loneliness.

But he has fallen into silence, and the silence is a warning. Klein is the last Jewish writer whom the rabbis and business-men will love. His silence marks the beginning of a massive literary assault on this community. Klein chose to be a priest though it was as a prophet that we needed him, as a prophet he needed us and needed himself. He moved through this community. He

3

watched honour migrate from the scholar to the manufacturer where it hardened into arrogant self-defense. Bronze plaques bearing names like Bronfman and Beutel were fastened to modern buildings, replacing humbler buildings established by men who loved books, in which their [sic] were no plaques at all.[b]

---

[a][The reference is to the line, "But touch not, Lord, the golden bowl!" in Klein's "Psalm XXII: A Prayer of Abraham, Against Madness" (*The Collected Poems of A.M. Klein,* comp. and introd. Miriam Waddington, Toronto: McGraw-Hill Ryerson, 1974, p. 223)].

[b][Crossed out:] Klein knew, felt, suffered the contempt

There is only one emotion which money has ever extended to idealism—contempt. Very early in my life I met men who lived and suffered under this contempt. They were the teachers in the Hebrew School I attended.[a] I am just beginning to understand why we never took them seriously, why their authority was so easily undermined. It was because our parents held them in

4

contempt. Because they were poor, because they were refugees, because they brought a broken, failed European past into this expensive synagogue, because they were shlemiels, that is scholars. They smelled of failure, and how shabby they seemed beside a glittering seat-owner. If ever a community succeeded in demonstrating its chosen values to its young - it was this community.[b] The whole learning apparatus was on the level of a charity function. Teachers wore the bitter, obsequious expression of men on welfare, (and I say in parentheses that we loved the one or two who dared to beat us) and our whole attendance had the atmosphere of an obligatory donation to U.J.A.,[c]

I will admit that the situation there was exaggerated because my synagogue was very rich, and none of its members had [made?] his fortune peddling the Talmud.

5

Klein saw this condition in communities across the country, but the Jews were under siege, so he became their clown. He spoke to men who despised the activity he loved most. He raised money. He chose to be a priest and to protect the dead ritual. And now we have his silence.

I do not think that any other writers from this community will make this mistake. They will prefer exile, the dialogue of the exile, a dialogue which seems to be very one sided, but it is still the old rich dialogue between the prophet and the priest, and

---

[a][Crossed out:] I had the impression
[b][Inserted between lines:],this opposition of wealth + humiliation.
[c][Crossed out:] more

the larger idea of community includes both of the parties.

The nominal community will continue to dismiss its writers and award them

6

the title of traitor. But the writers will continue to use the word 'Jew' in their poems, and so will be bound in the fascination which the nominal community has for this word.

"But I am not lost

perhaps an explanation of 'the nominal community

the British square
but there is nothing in the centre
what they preserve is themselves
their institution, their charities
their state within a state -
a
and no one can quarrel with the logic of survival
but there are men who must leave that square so as to produce those values for which the square was invented to enclose + protect

---

[C. Seven pages, marked a-f; two pages are marked as "e":]

a

History is the description of the path of an idea, a description of an idea's journey from generation to generation

I believe that at the beginning of an idea, each of the men who hold it[b] is both a prophet and a priest, but that as the

---

[a][Crossed out:] certain Jews
[b][Inserted between lines:] (and they are very few)

149

energy of the idea diminishes it, the functions of priest and prophet tend [?] to differentiate and soon no one man can perform both offices. As the idea exhausts itself in failure,[a] in combat with competing ideas—the[b] function of the prophet becomes irreconcilable to the function of the priest.

The priest is the archetype of the community which the original idea called into being. The community is marked with fossils of the original energy, and, convinced that only adherence to the original forms of

b

the idea, can rejuvenate it. The community is like an old lady whose canary has escaped in a storm, but who continues to furnish the cage with food + water + trapezes in the convinced hope that the canary will come back. The priest tries to persuade her that this optimism is religion.[c]

The prophet, on the other hand, continues to pursue the idea as it changes forms, trying never to mistake the cast off shell with the swift changing thing that shed it. He follows it into regions of danger, so that he becomes alive [or: alone?], and by his nature becomes unwelcome to the community. The community is a museum of the old form and dedicated to it, and changes very slowly, and usually only under violence.

c

Some moment in time, very brief, there must have been, among the ancient Hebrews, men who were both prophet + priest in the same office. I tease my imagination when I try to conceive of the energy of that combination. Their lives burned with such an intensity that we here can still feel [tell?] the warmth. I love the Bible because it honours them.

---

[a][Inserted between lines:] [illegible] absorption into the masses
[b][crossed out:] personality of
[c][Crossed out:] keeps telling her that her optimism

By the time this idea seized Moses it was no longer young, and he needed to create an elaborate law to bind himself to the community - for he was a prophet and he must [have] been anguished by the[a] distance growing between himself + the community.

When he smashed the tablets he signaled to all who followed him the futility of his project, and the anguish of knowing that,

d

even so, he is bound to persist in it.

I do not know what that original idea was, whose path through the generations was attended with such beauty and terror.

I want to know. On those rare occasions when I have purified myself I have intimation. Once I thought I was close and wrote this.

The Glass Dog [double underline]

I have tried to[b] offer a definition of history. Now I shall try to define idea.[c] Idea is the tongue of creation. It is the noise creation makes. It is the irresistible tune which we must follow like [illegible] follows theme in a symphony. Just as History is

e [several times altered]

the biography of idea, idea is the Birth Notice and Obituary of creation. It is the language of energy.

Well, you see how I have failed in my definition. All I know is that some men have drawn close to it, and have lived in its fire, and they are burning still.

I believe they beheld a unity, a barbarous finality, a vision of completion which their individual personalities could not resist,

---

[a][Crossed out:] sense
[b][Crossed out:] describe
[c][Crossed out:] I will confuse myself with

so they surrendered them. They became the idea, or as the Christians say, the word became flesh.

Thus they ventured into loneliness. Owning nothing, they could witness the divinity of everything. I know very little

e [sic]

about this. I have tried to discipline myself, to prepare myself, but I've only gone so far as arrogance - an attitude which is not nutritious.

I believe the idea concerned the sense of universal holiness, of the incorruptibility of creation, of the indissoluble community of all that exists.

Whatever it was we still feel its power and we have a very special treatment we [illegible] for those men who today move toward the idea, who tap [?] its energy - we force them into the solitude of leading us, or we exile them or kill them.

In my arrogance I wish to [illegible] their[a] shadows, rather than [illegible][b]

f

I am glad to be alone
a man must me [sic] very alone
before he can declare:
    We are not alone

As[c] Jews we are[d] afraid to be alone
Their[e] prophets[f] tell us[g] that we[h] are alone

---

[a][Inserted between lines:] huge
[b]Inserted at bottom of the page:] the blinding shadows of the community.
[c][Crossed out:] Now the
[d][Inserted between lines:] have become
[e][Overwritten:] The [? or:] Our [?]
[f][Crossed out:] writers
[g][Crossed out:] them
[h][Crossed out:] they

that all our[i] possessions create only loneliness,[j]
that they must be lonely with the awe of creation
before they can exult
    We are not alone
and claim to bring that triumphant message to the world
    before they can believe they give their destiny's, like a
child's gift, to the endless reflecting stars.

[D. One unmarked page in different ink; at least one preceding page is missing]

that Judaism was the faith which proclaimed the unity of God, and that all the [illegible]. I have conceived this discussion to concern the survival of monotheism in N.A.

I do not believe the philosophy has much of a chance. I think we have eliminated all but the most [illegible] + blasphemous ideas of God. I believe that the God worshipped in our synagogues is a hideous distortion of a supreme idea - and deserves to be attacked and destroyed. I consider it one of my duties to expose [illegible] platitude which we have created.

---

[i][Crossed out:] the
[j][Inserted between lines:] the paralyzing loneliness

WINFRIED SIEMERLING

A Political Constituency that Really Exists in the World: An Interview with Leonard Cohen

The interview took place in a coffee shop in North York on November 2, 1990 (and thus prior to the release of *The Future* and the publication of *Stranger Music*). Leonard Cohen had been staying at a hotel there in order to be close to his son, who had been hospitalised in North York after an accident.

Winfried Siemerling: You were about to come out with a new collection of poetry?

Leonard Cohen: I was. But I withdrew it.

WS: Why?

LC: I was not really satisfied. First of all I felt no urgency to put a book out, at this moment—although it would be nice, I suppose, to have a large *Collected Poems* around. But even that failed to really invigorate me as a project. I was urged by several people, including Jack McClelland and Adrienne Clarkson, to put out such a book, and I actually went to work for several months to determine what the content of such a book would be, and I also wanted to publish a lot of my songs. Well, I did all the work, and I came up with three books, a short book, a middle-sized book, and a long book. I established this index, and the long book was prepared. It's done, it's finished, but at a certain point I lost interest in the project. I thought it should have a preface. I thought it should have something else besides the poems and the songs, and then I became distracted with other matters.

WS: A similar process seems to have occurred with *Death of a Lady's Man* [1978]?

154

LC: It's chronic.

WS: The last book you have published is *Book of Mercy* [1984], and since then only records have appeared. What is the urgency you feel at certain points of your life to do certain projects, and what is the kind of community you want to address? At this point, music seems to be more important?

LC: I have never made a very distinct separation in my mind between music and writing. As I have said somewhere else, I have always felt that there was some kind of invisible guitar behind all my writing anyhow. Now I feel there is some kind of invisible synthesizer. But in my own consideration the work I've done in the last two years, or I would say perhaps since *Various Positions* [1984], contains some of the writing I'm most pleased with. So in a way, I don't feel at all that I've turned away from writing, because the lyrics on those two last records are about as accomplished as I feel I've gotten. In that sense there is no repudiation of literature or writing or the art of verse.

WS: When do you decide whether something will be a song lyric or a poem?

LC: I haven't been really interested in writing verse that is designed to sit on the page. I do not really know why that is. Writing music and making records and doing concerts involves me in the world in a way I like, which writing, especially writing verse, doesn't. It is a matter of loneliness. The writing of the material is solitary, it involves a great deal of solitude. At the end of that time I know I will be able to record and to put together a band again, which involves me with people. Actually, touring gives you the feeling of being part of a motorcycle gang. I don't want to miss those pleasures of the road.

WS: It seems to me that you have always had a very loyal and dedicated audience particularly in Europe, perhaps at times more so than in North America?

155

LC: Well, you don't really live in the echo of a career. When you're working continually, your work is in front of you. If you have any understanding of the market place at all you know that there are going to be moments when you are going to be valued, and you know that there are going to be moments when you are ignored if you're in it for the long haul, as I've always felt I would be from the very beginning. Of course you want to be praised and loved—but if you're not there is much in the enterprise itself to keep you interested. I think it's generally understood that European audiences are more loyal for a number of reasons. The market place here is glutted with material. Also the racking procedures, the way a singer's past work is kept in the stores is a phenomenon that exists almost only in Europe now, and it changes rapidly there as well.

WS: I would like to turn to some of your older work and ask you questions concerning some of your unpublished manuscripts.

LC: If I remember any of them . . .

WS: First, I am interested in the manuscript for a speech in Montreal, entitled "Loneliness and History."

LC: That's right. Was it partially about A.M. Klein and partially about the separatist movement? Or was that another speech I gave?

WS: You do discuss A.M. Klein in that manuscript. Did you actually give this speech? That was in 1964?

LC: Yes. At the Jewish Public Library. I think this must have been shortly after A.M. Klein died. It was shortly after . . . I believe he committed suicide. I have a certain self-protective amnesia. I don't remember very much about that period. I think that speech came out of conversations between Irving Layton and myself. He knew A.M. Klein very well; he introduced me to him. I did not go to any of his readings, but I did meet him before he died. The

156

feeling we both had, if I can remember, was that A.M. Klein had somehow tried to reconcile himself to the community. That he had written speeches for the Bronfman's, that he had tried to be a lawyer, that he had tried to be a good guy, and an outstanding member of the community, and that this had created a terrible conflict in his psyche, which he somehow could not reconcile.

WS: You wrote that it struck you that A.M. Klein used the word "we" in certain poems where he should have used "I."

LC: I think I had a feeling of his investment in being a spokesman, his sense that there was a community, and that he had to defend it against all opposition. I understand his position much better now.

WS: In what way did your attitude change?

LC: Community is a lot more fragile than I understood then, and a lot more valuable, and to undertake the defense of a community is a high call and in no sense a betrayal of a personal destiny. That is more my position today, I would say. But I was a young man then, confronting, I suppose, the same problems as A.M. Klein, but choosing a radically different path than A.M. Klein had chosen.

WS: You mention the word "traitor" several times in that speech and you make a distinction between a prophet and a priest. You suggest that a priest is the one who describes the path of an idea as history, whereas a prophet is the one who goes out and is alone, is by himself, and who is therefore not always welcome to a community. I thought that distinction was very interesting, especially in the light of what you say now.

LC: I was stimulated by those ideas in those days. I am not so stimulated by them now.

WS: Where did those ideas come from at the time?

LC: Those were the kinds of things my friends and I talked about. I think that those were pressing problems for many of us, as we were trying to decide how to lead our lives. Those were the natural kinds of conversations we had in those days because the matters themselves were pressing, were urgent.

WS: In what respect?

LC: What kind of life were we going to live? How were we going to make a living? How were you to protect your sense of integrity? Those were important matters then, and those are important matters now for anybody writing. Perhaps they were a little self-dramatizing at the moment, looking back on them now. But at the time they didn't seem at all that way. I think they are the legitimate and urgent concerns of a young writer. An older writer has different pressing concerns. In terms of being a Jewish writer at the time, A.M. Klein's life, his story, his achievement, his end—these were very serious matters to us, because he was the leading Jewish writer at the time and the fact that he had come to this particular moment in his life where it was no longer supportable was a matter of some gravity to us.

WS: You suggested that these matters have lost some of their direct importance now?

LC: I don't want to characterize them as unimportant; they just don't concern me at this moment. I've become a different person than I was in those days.

WS: Where has it shifted in terms of community? What seems important now?

LC: This conversation is interesting to me since I have been living more or less between a hotel room and a hospital room for the past three months and I haven't given much attention to these matters. I would say that the song "Tower of Song" touches on most of my urgent concerns at the moment. I suppose that the new songs I am working on are always closer to the position . . . although I do not consider myself as having a position at this point.

WS: "Tower of Song" speaks about loneliness and the question of who is supposed to answer. What is the situation in that song?

LC: I think it is in your work . . . since the rest of your life you cannot seem to be able to organize in any coherent manner. I think that everybody finds himself somewhere in the midst of a disaster as they approach middle age or late middle age. I think the ecological disaster is only an expression of the psychic disaster that is overtaking us all. We all find ourselves in the midst of some crisis that I have been talking about for many, many years as the Flood. We are in the midst of a flood. This time it's in the inner landscape where everything has been swept away and we are all clinging to pieces of orange crate and tops of tables. What is the appropriate behavior in the Flood as you pass other people in the stream? How do you greet other people in the midst of this disaster? My work more or less is an expression of the appropriate etiquette that we have towards one another in the midst of the disaster. That's mostly what I think my work is about. And trying to protect what can be protected, trying to discover appropriate greetings and salutations in a period when it is very difficult to locate any kind of form.

WS: Is it your sense that people don't affirm things anymore, or that they don't salute other people in the right way?

LC: It is difficult under these kinds of pressures to maintain a sense of etiquette. In other words, people have abandoned their manners. It is difficult to lead a courteous life under the circumstances in which we find ourselves. But in Toronto they manage to do it. People are very cordial.

WS: More so than in New York or Montreal?

LC: Well in Montreal you have a racial crisis. We've always had a situation which could be described as racial in Montreal, between all the groups. Now, because in the world at large the lid has been blown off and people feel this is the moment to struggle decisively for their own rights, naturally the cordiality has evaporated between the racial groups and we find ourselves in a confrontational period. In Montreal, you have to spend the first few seconds or moments of every encounter determining, first of all, which language you are going to speak. This runs quite deep. A great deal of energy is spent trying to establish a situation in which you do not murder each other.

WS: How did you feel about the situation at Oka? There is also an island named after Catherine Tekakwitha there.

LC: Catherine Tekakwitha's tomb is in what used to be called Caughnawaga. Since I didn't have to drive home every night to Châteauguay, I could afford to place my sympathies with the Mohawks.

WS: But you're saying that someone who did have to drive . . .

LC: Of course. You cannot expect people to embrace even a noble cause if their business and private lives are going to be disrupted for many, many weeks. It is almost impossible to choose sides today for someone so ambivalent as yours truly. Every side seems to have some real reasons . . . and it is not a joke. The rights of the Mohawks are not a joke. The rights of people who live under the incredible economic and social pressures that we all find ourselves in today . . . it is not a joke to be five hours on the road to get home. I do not have any skill in arbitrating these matters. It is interesting that *Beautiful Losers*, which was written in 1964, contains the essential material for the current situation: the Mohawks and the separatist contrast, which people did not take seriously at all. I remember saying around that time, I thought it was in the "Loneliness and History" speech, that blood is going to flow in the streets. I actually used that expression. I was addressing an English community and they thought this would never come to a head.

WS: Is Tekakwitha still a real spiritual power among Mohawks?

LC: If you go to Caughnawaga, almost everything is named Tekakwitha: the skating rink, the swimming pool, the high school—everything there is named for her. Her tomb is in the little church there. I do not know what spiritual force she has in that community.

WS: What meaning does she have for you? The speaker in *Beautiful Losers* begins with the words, "Catherine Tekakwitha, who are you?" Did she ever answer that speaker, or did she ever tell you?

LC: I have a statue of her on my stove in my house in Montreal. She is one of my household spirits. I think she embodied in her own life, in her own choices, many of the complex things that face us always. She spoke to me. She still speaks to me. There's a very beautiful bronze statue of her in front of the St. Patrick's Cathedral in New York City. I used to put some flowers there.

WS: With respect to the uncertainty that surrounds the figure of Catherine Tekakwitha and the speakers in the novel, reading *Beautiful Losers* reminded me to some extent of reading, for instance, Michael Ondaatje's [later] *Coming Through Slaughter*, which "is about" Buddy Bolden, the jazz musician who was never recorded. Ondaatje starts with a picture and he gives you many stories about Buddy Bolden, but in the end the reader is left with much uncertainty about both the speaker in the novel and Bolden. I had the impression a similar thing happens with Tekakwitha and whoever it is that speaks to and about her in your book. Now, in the case of *Beautiful Losers*, at least some of the early critics did not seem to be comfortable with that uncertainty.

LC: I don't really remember the book, but I remember the

161

writing of it. And I remember reading something in Dennis Lee's book [*Savage Fields*] where he said that this was on the way to becoming one of the greatest books ever written and somehow there was a failure of courage, of nerve, at some place in the book, and that after that it was downhill all the way. And I remember reading that and saying, "That's good, maybe that's right." On the other hand, I remember that I didn't feel that in the writing of it. If anything, it gathered momentum as it went along. I don't feel disposed to defend the book as it stands. I think people still read it out of interest and that's good enough for me.

I'm grateful for anybody spending any intellectual energy at all on my work and I appreciate it. I'm usually informed by things that I read about my work. As I said, I was very much informed when I read Dennis Lee's book, and often when I read serious studies of my work I'm very much informed and I feel a sense of gratitude. Sometimes people will ask me how I feel about certain artists covering my songs. They'll ask me, "how did you like the Lounge Lizards' version of 'Suzanne,'" or a punk version of a song, say Nick Cave's version of "Avalanche." I always answer that my critical faculties are suspended as soon as I hear that someone is doing one of my songs. I'm not there to judge it; I'm there to appreciate it. I like the idea that someone's doing one of my songs. I was sitting in here this morning and Jennifer Warnes' version of "Ain't No Cure For Love" came on and I was just delighted. We're in this world of writing and of ideas to delight and nourish ourselves, and I feel that I can embrace almost any position that doesn't have an unpleasant social repercussion, like theories of racial supremacy. Outside of those kinds of ideas, when I speculate on what an author means I find myself in a very objective position. I say "That's a good idea." I don't know whether that was my idea at the time. I don't feel attached to my ideas in that sense at all. I feel that they are speculations.

WS: But the process creates and transports a certain energy?

LC: That's a very good point. It produces energy, and as we've known for a long time, we're in the midst of an energy crisis. Well, I think it's the only way we can start to organize our lives, personal and civic, except I don't see how we can do it without that personal beginning of finding some kind of energy with which to confront our predicament. Certainly song used to do that.

WS: In her version of and response to "First We Take Manhattan," Jennifer Warnes, for instance, omits the two stanzas that appear in your later version, beginning with "And I thank you for those items that you sent me, the monkey and the plywood violin." What are the reasons for such differences?

LC: When I gave the song to Jennifer, I actually had already recorded my version, but I hadn't done the overdubs on it. She didn't like the bridge, "I'd really like to live beside you, baby," and I wrote many other bridges for her, and that wasn't easy because it takes me a long time to write. So I worked very hard and came up with several different bridges that she might feel more comfortable with; she didn't understand the verse. Jennifer's a very, very honest person, and in our association over the years she always made it very clear when she just didn't get something. It didn't have anything to do with whether it was good or bad; she just didn't get it. And she said, "I just don't get this—so, will you rewrite it," and I said, "Yes, I will." Finally she said "Yours is better than the ones you've given me. I think I'm beginning to see what it means." But she herself confessed to me after her song had been recorded and actually been a hit, "I didn't get this song. Your version, I understand it now." This all is part of this world we're talking about where ideas have a certain kind of energizing effect. Also in the song "Ain't No Cure For Love," she sings a song completely different from the one I sing. She doesn't do my final verse and she does a different middle verse. She's one of the most diligent workers that I've ever come upon. Her reading of the verses of any song are really impeccable. There's

163

nobody that can bring a verse to life like she can. That's why she has to know what it means. She can't fake it.

WS: In "First We Take Manhattan," what was the difference? What was it you were interested in?

LC: I think my version of this song is a better reading of the material. I don't consider myself in the same league as Jennifer in terms of singing, of being able to present a song. I think she's almost without peer. But my song was really political, a certain demented manifesto, which addresses a constituency that really exists in the world, which cannot be defined by left or right, that is a radical perspective of a great many people, internationally, who feel that there is no—not that we want to dispense with the political process, on the contrary—but from a certain point of view, that there is no political expression that represents us, that the language, the rhetoric of politics today has become so divorced from anybody's feelings and heart that it invites a new and radical rhetoric which in a kind of humorous and demented and serious way I touch upon in "First We Take Manhattan." Who is we? It is that we, and I use Manhattan and Berlin as the two real poles.

[Two young fans come to the table]

FAN: Are you Leonard Cohen?

LC: Yes, I am. How are you?

OTHER FAN: Are you really Leonard Cohen?

LC: Yes. I have been for a long, long time.

FAN: I just finished reading *Beautiful Losers.*

OTHER FAN: Same here. I have your tape in my bag.

164

LC: That's very kind of you. Thank you.

[Fans leave.]

LC: So I guess they are still reading it. When I was giving a concert in Athens someone told me people were greeting each other by saying, in Greek, "First we take Manhattan," and then the other person would say, "Then we take Berlin," just as a greeting.

WS: The first time I heard one of your songs was when I walked down a street in France one summer, and someone had opened a window and was playing a record of "So Long Marianne." You could hear it through the neighbourhood. And then when you came out with *I'm Your Man*, the same thing happened again. And I hadn't heard your music in public spaces for ten years, since '75 or so.

LC: I was pretty well eclipsed for a good ten or fifteen years.

WS: I think a lot of people liked *I'm Your Man* because it is often very funny and ironic. What about that stanza beginning "I thank you for the items that you sent me, the monkey and the plywood violin," and then the other one that starts "remember me, I used to live for music; remember me, I brought your groceries in," lines that also make it a bit rougher than the version by Jennifer Warnes?

LC: The speaker in this song is that guy who has been refused. "Thank you for the items that you sent me, the monkey and the plywood violin"—the song addresses the attitude that this appetite for redemption or resurrection or a new beginning is a joke, that it is something that can be scoffed at, laughed at, ridiculed, humiliated. This appetite we have for resurrection of a value and meaningfulness was something, especially during the 80s, that was an object of contempt and scorn and ridicule. "Thank you for the items that you sent me"—people had that

165

appetite for monkeys or for organ grinders or for plywood violins. That's the kind of attention we gave to those kinds of spirits; they were foolish figures playing on makeshift instruments, they had no place and were deservedly outside of things. Those outsiders, that outsider in all of us, is the one who is speaking now. That's what we all hunger for, to be able to express that one that we put to the side, that we ourselves ridiculed. We all bought into another story—that we could live without that part of us.

WS: Who is the sender of the items?

LC: I tend to look at all the personages or the characters in the songs as being part of the same landscape, the interior landscape. The sender is the part of ourselves that diminished that voice that was asking for a . . . I don't want to set up an encompassing spirit . . . but that part of ourselves that was demanding a spiritual aspect to our lives was the one we ignored. And we gave that part of ourselves that was hungry some kind of perverse and obscene charity. We made him into an organ grinder, a plywood violin, a monkey, thanks a lot. Instead of giving that part of ourselves a throne, and a court, and a scepter, and a command, a perspective, a tower, we gave that part of us a monkey and a plywood violin, so that it would screech away and amuse us with its antics.

WS: Does the "we" here represent demands from the outside? Is it part of yourself?

LC: These things operate in many realms. In a certain sense, I feel most comfortable when I think of myself as the leader of a government-in-exile. Sometimes I like to think of myself that way. It gives me a position that I can work from. It is not whether I take it seriously or not seriously; we are not speaking about a rational operation. It is just that one feels that one can embody the unspoken aspirations, of both oneself and the people you know, as somebody who takes responsibility for the predicament,

166

and presents not a solution but at least an approach. That leads you to some interesting kinds of positions. In "Tower of Song" I take the position of someone who is going to last forever: "You will be hearing from me long after I'm gone." It does not matter if I believe in this, if I have any real investment in that position as the leader of a government-in-exile. That doesn't matter. It is a mode of thought.

WS: You use "Our Government-In-Exile" as a subtitle in a passage in *Death of a Lady's Man*. In that passage you also use a name that is spelled "Micjel".

LC: That is taking on a European kind of sensibility, which exists in Quebec in the political realm. The fact that revolution is a desirable idea, that things can be transformed, that there is movement, conspiracy, enemies. I wanted to have a name close to Michel, but that had that "j" that existed in European languages and that nobody ever knows how to pronounce.

WS: I'd like to ask you a few questions about another of your manuscripts, about that first unpublished novel, "A Ballet of Lepers." Where did you write it?

LC: I wrote it in 1957 or 1958 in my mother's house. I'm not quite sure of the dates. I graduated from McGill in 1955. I had not gone to Europe yet.

WS: What did you do with that novel? Did you send it off?

LC: I was mostly interested in publishing in paperback in those days. I was never interested in those days in conventional publishers.

WS: You were thinking of one of the small presses?

LC: No, I was thinking of a huge division. Paperbacks were not as fancy as they are today. There were not really any trade paperbacks, they were all just in drugstores and airports. That was the market I was interested in. But I only got rejections.

WS: Where did you send it?

LC: I sent it to, maybe, Pocketbooks and a pocketbook company called Ace Publications, something like that. I think I sent it just to two.

WS: What do you think of it now?

LC: I do not know what it was about. I don't remember anything at all about it. You know, we probably write the same thing over and over again. Again, I remember the writing of it, because I had a clock on my desk, and I forced myself to write a certain number of hours every day and I watched this clock. It had no glass on it and I always thought I could just move the hand with my finger. I remember writing on the face of the clock the word "help."

WS: Is this something you feel you would like a broader public to have access to?

LC: I have hundreds and hundreds of pages of unpublished material and I don't have any sense of urgency about it. I feel I've written it and maybe one day, if it concerns anybody, it will come to light. I think posthumously would be a good time to publish these. If ever a scholar arises who is deeply interested in the matter, there are hundreds and hundreds of pages, and among those hundreds of pages there are a few that are worthwhile. But I can't even decide among the published work what is worthwhile. That's one of the problems I had with putting a *Collected Poems* together. I really didn't feel like deciding what's worthwhile and what isn't. The other few hundred pages are the same thing: if the work still has some relevance in other generations maybe someone will put together a book like *The Crack-Up* by Fitzgerald, an anthology of his little snippets. I think Edmund

Wilson gleaned it from his papers, and they put together a beautiful little book.

Backstage at the Schlossberg in Graz, Austria, 1985
Photo by Gerhard Schinzel

JOHN SIMON

Dear Leonard—

Congratulations, or something . . .

Comparing you with the American "man-in-black", Johnny Cash's attire may be as sepulchral, but his poetic images don't hold a candle to the blackness of yours (or *do* hold 2 candles . . . whatever).

May your next 60 years be as bright as your darkest lyric is bleak.

SONJA A. SKARSTEDT

Let Us
for Leonard Cohen

Slow motion conjurings of oranges
like suns in a surrealist's dream
we offer our ears to a shepherd's song
down to a valley where the enemy
deposits all weapons in a river turning acid
to crystal blue, their once-barbarous hands
sculpting wildflowers from debris
come they call

let us waltz a mending waltz
let us celebrate this cactus earth
let us infiltrate structure
with sensuous intentions

In unison we pull down conduits
of wind, silk flags shaped
                    from the stalks of tattered countries
wind them over our imperfect bodies
all sizzle all fusion we saturate
the cosmos, creating an alpha
                    in these trembling ruins

examining the manifold creases
in a human palm, we shut
our eyes and ears into roselike
                    omegas
leaving only the mouth
its *subconscious*
            cinematic
                    amplifications.

RAYMOND SOUSTER

Through A Fog Of Remembrance
for the Spice-Box Man

1.

These notes tell me you read
on October 31, 1959,
in our Contact Readings, Third Series,
held at Av Isaacs'
Bay-Gerrard Greenwich Gallery
on the edge of Toronto's two-block "Village",
with 120 people in attendance
(of whom 97 paid a quarter each),
and more turned away at the door—
it would never happen again.

Looking quite serious you told us
that you couldn't play your guitar that evening
(and therefore wouldn't be singing),
because you'd snapped
a string that you couldn't replace
until you got back to Montreal.
And while you spoke we first noticed
one little pouch made of cotton
tied somehow to each inside sleeve
of your brown corduroy jacket.

And believe it or not, Leonard Cohen,
my good wife and I
are still debating today
what you said (if in fact you said),
those two pouches contained
and why you took them everywhere
(for good luck Lia thinks you may have told us).

Of course I can't ask you now—
that time's at least a couple
of centuries behind us—
and who knows, your memory
of an "old" man of sixty,
may not be much better
than our joint memories here,
both with three-score-and-tens
soon to stretch behind us.

2.

Now Lia recalls
an early visit to your city,
when we went with Louis Dudek
to see you perform
at an upstairs coffee house downtown,
whose name we can't remember any more,

only retain the gist of your words
as you explained the reason
for the dark bruise above your eye:
you'd been sitting with a girl at intermission
sipping coffee, when her boy-friend
just happened by, walked up to your table
and without any warning at all
tried to punch your lights out,
coming very close, you said, to succeeding.

And while I can't be sure,
I'd be almost willing to bet
that by comparison
your countless gigs since that night
have been largely unspectacular.

3.

That last time I saw you
Earle Birney and I,
after lunch at *Gasthaus Schroeder*,
walked back to Yonge Street,
then, were almost at Dundas,
when a figure in a leather jacket
flashed by in the crowd,
and I was so sure it was you
that I yelled out "Leonard!"
and you turned around,
must have recognized the two of us,
because your solemn face managed a smile,
and the three of us ended up
making polite, awkward talk over coffee,
shortly after went our separate ways;

Earle for my money still the reigning champ,
me, an also-ran contender,
you, the new heir-apparent,
with one thing at least we could agree on:
that the name of the game was still poetry,
and nothing else really mattered
but our lifetime allegiance
to that totally demanding goddess,
more a slut than a lady at times!

Much later that day I must confess
I thought of offering up a solemn prayer
to the goddess for the three of us,
asking that the pure gift of poetry
bless us while breath remained
in our unworthy bodies;
but held back, finally deciding
that I had no business meddling
in the lives of others.

So tell me now, Leonard
(much too late of course),
did I do right that day
or instead fumble on the one-yard line?

Of course I'll understand
if silence is your chosen answer.

PHIL SPECTOR

"I would be remiss . . ."

I would be remiss, if I did not mention at this time, one particular person, poet and artist, who confessed to me that he was extremely influenced by the Partridge Family. And that artist is Leonard Cohen. Underneath that brooding, moody, depressed soul which Leonard possesses, lies an out-and-out Partridge Family freak. He never misses their re-runs on Nickelodeon; belongs to their fan club; and for lack of a more appropriate word, is a Partridge Family "groupie," albeit, one who still remains "in the closet" in connection with these feelings. May I suggest you contact him, and I am sure he will provide you with much in-depth information as to how profound was the way in which the Partridge Family influenced every facet of his personal and professional life.

ALAN TWIGG

The Maple Leaf Forever

In recent years I broke up with Joni, but I remain faithful to
Leonard. Leonard Cohen and I go way back. He was my musical
best man back in the eleventh grade. That was the year Tara
came to our high school. We would sit on the floor of her
parents' living room listening to Leonard Cohen droning on the
hi-fi, smoking Old Port wine-tipped cigarillos. I would serenade
her with barely passable renditions of "Suzanne" and "Hey, That's
No Way To Say Goodbye." I still can't fingerpick properly. But I
intend to be of enormous value in the nursing home when we're
all on rocking chairs, trying desperately to recall the final verse
of "One Of Us Cannot Be Wrong".

Leonard was a poet that we knew. John Grierson's National
Film Board documentary, "Ladies and Gentleman, Leonard
Cohen", confirmed that Leonard was cool. He was a bond be-
tween us all. He and Joni Mitchell. They were Canadian singer-
songwriters who were quite simply deeper, more poetic, more
exploratory. It made you proud to know this 'literary' style of
making music came from north of the U.S. border. It was a level
of communication I aspired to, that led me into adulthood.

Tara and I were married. I became a literary journalist. I kept
writing songs, playing in a band. Leonard came to town for an
interview. It was like meeting an old friend. I immediately felt I
could go down the street and shoot a game of pool with this guy.
This was during his "Death of a Lady's/Ladies Man" era. I re-
lated to his Eeyore world view. He said many memorable things
that day, my favourite being 'A book is a small thing in this
world'. Our conversation was sincere. It wasn't simply an exer-
cise. In those days I could still ask genuine questions. I loved his
sense of humour.

Afterwards I called Tara and we all went for a walk in Stanley
Park. We ate popcorn at English Bay. We have photographs. In
retrospect, there was something ceremonial going on. Dressed

in a dark suit, as always, Leonard was a ministerial figure. Although he didn't know us beforehand, he acted as if he did. We weren't fans, we were friends. Unlike many authors I've met, he was curious about what we had to say. Our brief triad was a confirmation of paths taken.

Leonard posed obediently for pictures. I've met hundreds of authors—most of the so-called 'major' ones in Canada during the 1970s and early '80s—but only Leonard Cohen and Pierre Berton know how to have their pictures taken. They immediately become co-conspirators. Leonard and I were standing side-by-side when Leonard picked up a large maple leaf. He twirled it then slipped its stem under his belt. He became Adam. It was a spontaneous joke. He posed blank-faced. As Canadian as maple syrup.

I still have that photo. It's the only photo I keep on my office wall. There's my pal, Leonard Cohen, with a maple leaf covering his crotch. I'm the intrepid, shoddily-dressed, squinting young journalist who shouldn't be in the same picture.

Since then we crossed paths on his *Book Of Mercy* tour. That meeting was a confirmation of the first. He was dressed the same. He kindly said he remembered me. Strangely, it didn't much matter to me whether this was true or not. I've been to a concert, bought a few records, kept track of him in the news. Nothing special. But our long-distance relationship endures. I appreciate his work. Now my teenage son is at the same age I was when I met his mother. From the basement, amid blasts of Pearl Jam and the Screaming Trees, I often hear Leonard's voice. My sons' friends like him, they dig the words. He is, apparently, still cool.

This is uplifting. To know that Leonard endures. To know that I have chosen wisely in my artistic influences. So it is that we remain loyal, hundreds of thousands of us. When I was a theatre critic for CBC Radio in the early 1980s I gave the news to the show's producer that Leonard Cohen was coming to town and we could interview him. She told me Leonard Cohen was boring. It was my cue to quit the show.

The world is divided. Some of us are inspired by the fact that Leonard has been able to maintain a consistently artistic out-

178

Leonard Cohen in Stanley Park, Vancouver, with Alan Twigg, 1978
Photo by David Boswell

look. Coming from a young country like Canada, which distrusts art and artists, this practically qualifies Leonard for sainthood. It is a brave and rare thing, to function as Leonard has. He is not known as an intellectual. He eschews politics. He does not teach Creative Writing. He prefers to be photographed eating a banana. Or posing with a maple leaf. Adamite.

Many people have written wise and penetrating views of Leonard Cohen and his work. I am thankful to be able to pay tribute. Thanks, Leonard. Our household thanks you. Our street thanks you. Our neighborhood thanks you. You are in our hearts. You are in our basements. We're proud of you. You have given us much pleasure. (For a desert island classic, I'd probably pick "Song of Bernadette", Jennifer Warnes' version.) When you're dead, we'll dangle icons of you from rear view mirrors.

JENNIFER WARNES

Jenny Sings Lenny

One evening late in the spring of 1986 Leonard Cohen made this sketch on a white paper placemat at Mario's Italian Restaurant in Hollywood, California. Work was in progress on a new as yet untitled recording of my interpretations of nine of Leonard's songs. He had surprised me that day with a visit to the studio and my work as I recall went better, as it often did when he appeared.

Everyone involved with this project loved Leonard's music in the purest way. I believe because of that, we were oddly blessed. Mid-project as we were, it was still too soon to celebrate, but we quietly percolated with the suspicion that something extraordinary was being born. Later that evening, Leonard and I left the studio for an early dinner where we allowed ourselves to rejoice a little about our progress, and to muse about the cover art. In this spirit, Leonard set his dinner plate aside, pulled a pen from his breast pocket, and this sketch appeared quickly on the paper mat. Eventually, however, the album came to be titled "Famous Blue Raincoat" after his song of the same name. I felt this image was more powerfully his because when I first met him in Hartford in '69, he was something of a trench-coated dark angel on the prowl.

But, that's not the whole story. To me, this little drawing was sacred and private, and I secretly resisted turning it into an advertisement. Leonard, however, has never forgiven me for not using it as the cover. But among those of us who worked on this recording, of which I am deeply proud, this is, in fact, the true cover and unofficial title.

PHYLLIS WEBB

Tibetan Desire

That night, did I wear red nailpolish? If I did, it wasn't called
"Tibetan Desire." That was the name of the nailpolish F. chose in
Beautiful Losers—"such a contradiction in terms"—to paint a plas-
tic model of the Akropolis red, with the tiny brush.

It "gleamed like a huge ruby" as the narrator and F. lay look-
ing at it in the glow of the soft morning beyond, and when they
squinted "it burst into a cool lovely fire, sending out rays in all
directions. . . Don't weep, F. said, and we began to talk."

It was the sixties. I was in Montreal for some reason I now
forget, not the Chelsea Hotel, not the Akropolis either. Leonard
had come to guide me through my first unnatural high. Was I
wearing red nailpolish? Was I going to see the world as a huge
ruby bursting into fire?

We lit up. You've got to see Ste. Catherine Street, L said. And
then we'll go and have Chinese food. It tastes fantastic.

Nothing's happening.

It will.

I puffed. He waited patiently. Not the Chelsea Hotel. Not a
huge ruby. A grid moving on my right shoulder blade, a *grid*,
eyes at the back of my head. You're there, you're high, or some
such words. Giggling, conspiratorial, we set out for the cool
night beyond. We wandered along the sainted street reacting to
movie posters, shop windows, people, neon signs, happy, hun-
gry, elevated, heading for the ultimate taste sensation of Montreal
Chinese food.

I'd first met L back in the fifties at Irving Layton's house in
Côte St. Luc. Louis Dudek had brought his protegé at the time
they were preparing *Let Us Compare Mythologies* for Contact Press.
I remember being surprised to learn that Leonard, who seemed
so young, was voluntarily studying the Bible as an informal on-
going project. How that old Christian fascination has kept pace

with his consciousness de-formations still puzzles me, is still insistently summoned, rock of ages, in his latest album, *The Future*.

Who was there? Or who was usually there, because I don't remember the exact line-up the night of L's arrival. Betty Layton, of course, radiant and smiling, always a luminous presence, and a wonderful friend to me; the Layton children, Maxie and Naomi (Sissyboo), and Irving, who tried to sell us his latest books, who read his spectacular poems. Miriam Waddington occasionally appeared, and Frank Scott, Al Purdy, Gael Turnbull, Eli Mandel, Avi Boxer, Aileen Collins, Louise Scott, Robert Currie, others. The Layton living-room was small, but it never felt crowded; the talk was lively and spontaneous, poems got batted about, L's being the most freshly lyrical and genuinely sensuous, I think I thought. Leonard was trying Law School at McGill, though he'd soon drop out. It must have felt strange to him to have Frank Scott, professor of constitutional law, greet him in such an informal setting. But our youngest poet was even then suave and cool and collected, on the outside, at least. There's always been a space around him. Sometimes it lets you in, sometimes it doesn't.

I was soon to leave for a year in London, but when I came back I saw Leonard from time to time. One night we'd gone out for a drive and ended up at his mother's house where he was staying. That's when he introduced me to mangoes and talked about the young woman he was in love with. I wrote a poem about the mango experience, revising it some years later:

REVISION

I slice the flesh of an old poem
I started for you in 1957
called "Mangoes for Leonard Cohen"
the lines fall away
flesh that is often lost

Now I slice into the luminous
mangoes like a surgeon

184

the delight in my eyes
as they behold the broken tissue
is the delight of the skilful surgeon. . . .

My other recollections are of the more professional times we
spent together in Toronto when I worked for the CBC. Memo-
ries of having coffee at the Four Seasons Hotel across the street
from the studio when L showed me the notebook he always
carried with him, the poems and songs, the multiple revisions.
Listening to him and watching as he recorded poems for the
1966 CBC two LP album *Canadian Poets I.* Another time there
was a private concert at the Park Plaza Hotel when he sang
"Dress Rehearsal Rag", saying he'd never record it. He did, in
Songs of Love and Hate in 1971.

In 1967, Centennial year, I was doing a series of television
programs on contemporary Canadian poetry for the CBC and
brought Leonard and Gwen McEwen together for a half-hour
program. I thought it was a dazzling combination. Both of them
beautiful and "exotic", both spice-box of earth poets, both myste-
rious and seductive, regional only in their universality. The pro-
grams were shown at some miserably early hour on Sunday morn-
ings.

I think this professional connection must have begun in
Montreal when I interviewed Leonard for CBC radio just after he
had returned from Europe where he'd written *Beautiful Losers.*
He was still recovering from that experience and I saw a dramatic
change in him—a wilder, more battered L, sunstroked from
writing outside in the Grecian light.

The radio and TV meetings ended when I left the CBC in
1969 and returned to the west coast. So did our friendship. I
never heard from him again.

But recently (summer, 1993) he re-entered my consciousness
very powerfully. He was scheduled to give a concert in Victoria,
B.C. on June 29th at the Royal Theatre. I'd never actually seen
him in concert and I decided I must go. Stephen Scobie was able
to nab a ticket for me and a pass for backstage after the show. It
was a great evening, a great concert promoting *The Future,* the

185

visual effects reminding me of German Expressionist painting (I've seen the past and it is murder). He didn't seem to recognize me when we met, which seemed so strange as to be laughable. It had *only* been 25 years or so since we'd seen each other, after all. He got the scene right, though: Montreal, Irving's house, Betty Layton, a key reference, so many dead. Perhaps he just couldn't recall my name after a European tour and a three hour songfest. Or just refused to say Phyllis. (I never ever wanted to call him Len or Lennie).

But that was not the end of it. There was Helga. I'd been billetted at her home when I was attending a conference in Essen a few years ago. Helga is what you call a fan, of Cohen's, of Canada. In the Canada Suite in her house she has a signed photo of him, along with autographed photos of Omar Sharif, Brian Mulroney and Mila, Pierre Trudeau, Joe Clarke and Maureen, etc. Leonard is, I suspect, Helga's soul-mate, his songs an accompaniment to her life as wife, mother, former fashion model, executive member of the German Canadian Society in Dusseldorf. Suddenly, Helga decides to visit me at the end of July after delivering some exchange students to Toronto. And Leonard Cohen will be doing a return engagement in Victoria on July 30th, I tell her. It's her 30th wedding anniversary, but her husband is understanding, and her daughter encourages her to take this opportunity because she missed the *Future* concert when L was in Germany. Stephen Scobie is rounded up to work his magic at getting tickets (he'd also stayed in the Canada Suite on one of his jaunts). He's able to seat her in the front row and take her backstage to meet L. She will present him—as she's done in 1988 at his *I'm Your Man* concert in Montreal—a single red rose, glowing like a huge ruby.

That night when I was either wearing red nailpolish or not wearing red nailpolish, on the way back to the hotel I fell into a depression L was concerned about because, he said as we parted, a marijuana low is really serious. But I was used to depression, no doubt more comfortable with natural lows than unnatural highs. He didn't say, "Don't weep." He hadn't written that book yet. I

186

was touched by his attentiveness to my mood change and grateful for his sense of responsibility as guide on my round about trip.

After the June 29th concert, backstage, I thought Leonard exhibited an extraordinary Buddhistic calm, the space around him larger, more defined now by professional distance. Stephen thought he was just plain tired. You still don't remember me, I teased. Of course I do, darlin'. I wasn't quite convinced, something hadn't clicked. Then the space collapsed briefly as he gave me a warm hug, his post-performance body-heat a cool lovely fire passing through me on its way to Tibet.

GEORGE WOODCOCK

Weary Day on Parnassus

It was a weary day
on Parnassus
and I washed my feet
in the Castalian spring
regarding that safer
than drinking.

Yet in that cool crystal,
shallow over rock,
I heard the silent ripple
of words
and the drip drop drip under ferns
as thought kept its pool filled.

And waited for the fish of vision
that never came.

TIM WYNNE-JONES

Dear Leonard:

I failed high school English. But since I was going to be an architect, they passed me anyway. I loved the stuff we were studying: Hamlet—loved him. A crow flew into our class room while we were studying *Hamlet* and I tried to explain how that crow was part of the story. Somehow. Didn't get very far. Didn't know where I was going.

I loved *Heart of Darkness* and "Paul's Case", about the kid who steals the money from a movie theatre in Pittsburgh and runs off to New York to live the high life for a couple days, then kills himself and leaves a rose on the track—loved it. And Theodore Roethke. Argued with my teacher about him too. I wasn't smart, wasn't radical, wasn't chic. But I had a feeling. Or maybe I just had a nose for shit.

When I was being interviewed for architecture school, in order to see if I was "informed," they asked me, among other things, whether I'd heard of *The Spice Box of Earth*. And sure—I'd read about it in *Time* magazine. So I passed that test, okay.

Then at the University of Waterloo, in a house of boy engineers and architects in training and—mercifully—one English major, I heard "Suzanne." It was the first poem I ever got. I don't mean "understood;" don't even mean could analyze within an inch of its precious life; don't mean I could write a test on it. Maybe I knew I would never write a test like that again.

I got "Suzanne" in the blood.

They say we are completely new every seven years. It's been twenty-six years, but there is still a residue of her, Suzanne, on the shores of every cell of my body. She's washed up there for good. The tides don't seem to wash her away. Just clean her up a bit. Rearrange her hair.

It's great to have this opportunity to say thanks. For *Spice Box* and sweet Sue and *The Future*. Many happy returns of the day.

189

Contributors

JOAN BAEZ is a well-known recording artist. DOUGLAS BARBOUR teaches at the University of Alberta. BILL BISSETT paints and writes in Toronto. George Bowering's latest book is *The Rain Barrel.* ROBERT BRINGHURST lives in British Columbia. ADRIENNE CLARKSON is the host of *Adrienne Clarkson Presents.* ANDREI CODRESCU edits *Exquisite Corpse* and is a commentator for National Public Radio. JUDY COLLINS is well-known as a songwriter in her own right, and as an interpreter of Leonard Cohen's music. JOHN ROBERT COLOMBO is a prominent Canadian author and anthologist. LORNA CROZIER's most recent book is *Inventing the Hawk.* CHARLIE DANIELS plays a mean fiddle. BEA DE KONING and YVONNE HAKZE edit *Intensity.* JIM DEVLIN edits the *Leonard Cohen Information Newsletter.* ANN DIAMOND's latest book is *Evil Eye.* MARY DI MICHELE teaches creative writing at Concordia University. BARBARA DODGE first met L.C. in 1970. STAN DRAGLAND teaches at the University of Western Ontario. LOUIS DUDEK published Cohen's first book, *Let Us Compare Mythologies,* in the McGill Poetry Series. DOUGLAS FETHERLING has published over forty books and lives in Toronto. RAYMOND FILIP's most recent book is *Flowers in Magnetic Fields.* JUDITH FITZGERALD writes a column about C & W for the *Toronto Star.* MICHAEL FOURNIER is a bartender and editor. GARY GEDDES teaches at Concordia University. ALLEN GINSBERG teaches at Brooklyn College. CRISTOF GRAF has written the book-length study *So Long, Leonard.* RALPH GUSTAFSON lives in North Hatley, Quebec. NOEL HARRISON recorded "Suzanne" in 1967. JOY JOHNSTON first met L.C. in Nashville in 1970. TOM KONYVES lives in Vancouver. KRIS KRISTOFFERSON has a special affection for "Bird on the Wire." PATRICK LANE lives in British Columbia. DENNIS LEE's latest book is *Riffs.* GILLIAN MCCAIN writes and edits in New York City. JACK MCCLELLAND has published most of Cohen's books. DAVID MCFADDEN's latest book is *An Innocent in Ireland.* SEYMOUR MAYNE teaches at the University of Ottawa. PATRICIA MORLEY is the author of *As Though Life Mattered: Leo*

Kennedy's Story. SUSAN MUSGRAVE's most recent book is *Forcing the Narcissus.* IRA NADEL is the author of *Leonard Cohen: A Life in Art.* JOHN NEWLOVE's latest book is *Apology for Absence.* KEN NORRIS currently lives in Toronto. P.K. PAGE lives in British Columbia. AL PURDY is a well-known Canadian poet. HARRY RASKY made the film *The Song of Leonard Cohen.* STEPHEN SCOBIE is the author of *Leonard Cohen* and *Alias Bob Dylan.* WINFRIED SIEMERLING currently lives in Sherbrooke, Quebec. JOHN SIMON was the producer of *Songs of Leonard Cohen.* SONJA SKARSTEDT is the author of *Mythographies.* RAYMOND SOUSTER lives in Toronto. PHIL SPECTOR co-wrote and produced *Death of a Ladies' Man.* Alan Twigg lives in Vancouver. JENNIFER WARNES recorded *Famous Blue Raincoat,* an album of Cohen songs. PHYLLIS WEBB first met L.C. in Montreal in the 1950s. GEORGE WOODCOCK lives in Vancouver. TIM WYNNE-JONES loves the song "Suzanne."